The
Story of the Bible
from A to Z

STEFANIE BOYLES

STUDY CONTRIBUTORS

· ·

Designer:
KATIE LINSTRUM

Editor:
JANA WHITE

www.thedailygraceco.com

TABLE of CONTENTS

We can see throughout the Old Testament that God's people were waiting for Him to fulfill His promise of a coming Savior. They were given many clues to look out for: the Savior would come from the tribe of Judah (Gen. 49:10), in the town of Bethlehem (Mic. 5:2), from the line of David (Isa. 9:6-7). This promise of a Savior is actually first seen in the same chapter as the fall. As soon as God confronts Adam and Eve's disobedience, He declares judgment on the serpent and claims ultimate victory: "I will put hostility between you and the woman, and between your offspring and her offspring. He will strike your head, and you will strike his heel" (Gen. 3:15). The offspring of woman is a collective noun, which indicates a corporate victory that will be won by the incarnate Son of God, Jesus Christ, the Promised Savior for His people. But this promise wasn't fulfilled for generations. It was thousands of years before Christ entered the world. This waiting included a lot of corruption, war, rebellion, and depravity. There were cycles of disobedience, repentance, and mercy.

> *But then the promise was fulfilled when Jesus came as a helpless baby. In fact, all of the promises of God in the Old Testament were fulfilled in Him. Jesus lived a sinless life, died on the cross, and was resurrected from the dead. Through His death and resurrection, Jesus achieved victory over Satan. The first gospel message seen in Genesis 3:15 was fulfilled in Christ, and He offers that victory to His children, all for the glory of God.*

Fast forward two thousands years. As believers today, we enter a different season of waiting. We wait not for Jesus to return as a helpless baby, but for Him to return as a righteous judge. Now, we expectantly wait for a promised future that will come when Jesus returns to consummate the kingdom of God. But our season of waiting is different because we have the Holy Spirit. Our waiting is active because we have a mission to continue. Jesus came "to seek and to save the lost" (Luke 19:10), and we have the indwelling Holy Spirit to empower us to join in on God's work to do the same. Our season of waiting is in the tension of the "already, not yet." We have a taste of the sweetness of redemption in this life but the fullness will come at the consummation.

The stories may be familiar to you and your kids, but rather than pulling out moral lessons, they will point to the Promised Savior.

Seeing Jesus in the Old Testament reminds us that this was God's plan before the foundation of the world, and the Bible has a unified narrative of redemption through Christ. This unified narrative is the story of Scripture, and the aim of this devotional is to make it clear that this story is actually the story of Jesus. The gospel is Christological – from the Old Testament to the New Testament. This is what Jesus was saying in Luke 24 when He said everything in the Old Testament pointed to Him. A common phrase used to display the Christological focus in each individual narrative in Scripture is *true and better* – for example, Jesus is the *true and better Adam*. Because indeed, it was God's glorious plan to use every character in every smaller narrative to point to the One who is greater and the main character in the grand narrative. So it is helpful to use this phrase to communicate to kids that these familiar stories are part of the bigger story, and the hero of every story is Jesus.

It is also true that there are actual "types" of Christ in the Old Testament, like Moses. The idea of typology in the Bible is that certain persons and events in the Old Testament are divinely set in God's plan to prefigure a future fulfillment of His plan seen in the New Testament. The central hope of this devotional is to help you and your family discover Jesus in the Old Testament and understand that the stories in the Old Testament point to Jesus and find their completion in Him. So after we move through the Old Testament, we will go over the life, death, and resurrection of Jesus. The cross is the climax of God's story of redemption! He came and fulfilled the mission – just as He said He would! But what now? We'll end this devotional looking at the time after Jesus' ascension and the start of our current season of waiting for Jesus to come back.

Because the Promised Savior did come, we have reason to confidently wait for His promised return. May we celebrate as we reflect on God's faithfulness as seen in the fulfillment of His promise of a Savior. And may this reflection strengthen our hearts to persevere in our current season of waiting.

WE HAVE A MISSION TO CONTINUE SO MAY WE COUPLE OUR HOPEFUL EXPECTATION WITH ACTIVE PARTICIPATION IN THE LOCAL CHURCH AND IN OUR OWN FAMILIES.

A RESCUE STORY

The Bible begins with the story of how God created the world out of nothing and called it "good." Sadly, this didn't last long because God's creation, Adam and Eve, fell into the temptation of Satan and questioned God's goodness. Even though God gave them a beautiful garden to live in, they ate the one fruit God told them not to eat because they thought that God was not giving them the very best. Could God love them and still say "no" to something? (Do your parents say "no" to you, but still love you? Of course!)

But soon after Adam and Eve disobeyed God and sin entered the world, God declared that a Rescuer would come and defeat Satan. You see, God is holy, which means He is perfect and pure. He has never sinned and He never will sin. God loves His holiness and will not tolerate sin, which meant Adam and Eve needed help to pay the price for sin if they ever wanted to live in God's presence again. God knew this, and because He loved Adam and Eve, He told Satan right away that a Rescuer was going to come and defeat him.

I will put hostility between you and the woman,
and between your offspring and her offspring. He will
strike your head, and you will strike his heel.
GENESIS 3:15

God is kind and loving, and He gives Adam and Eve good news right away. In the middle of the curse, God gives a promise of a Rescuer, and this Rescuer would pay the price of sin and make a way for human beings to live in God's presence again. Satan would strike the Rescuer's heel, but the Rescuer would strike his head, which simply meant the Rescuer would claim victory over Satan. God wins and Satan loses.

The Rescuer in God's plan is Jesus, and this rescue story is the story of the Bible. You may have heard a lot of different stories from the Bible, but the point of all those stories is to point to Jesus. The Bible isn't just a book about a lot of heroes that we should try to be like. No, the Bible has stories of imperfect heroes that show our need for the perfect hero, Jesus.

Jesus wasn't plan B. There was never a plan B. Jesus was the plan — the one and only plan. Before God created the world out of nothing, He knew the whole story. God made humans in His image and our beautiful earth and the big universe all for His glory, which just means His unmatchable greatness and worth. And His rescue story, which is the big story of the Bible, is all for His glory, too.

THE RESCUER IN GOD'S PLAN IS JESUS,
AND THIS RESCUE STORY IS THE STORY OF THE BIBLE.

PRAY TOGETHER AS A FAMILY

Dear God,

Thank You that You are good, kind, and loving. Thank You for giving us Jesus, the perfect hero, to save us from our sins. Thank You that this was Your plan all along. You were not surprised by sin, and You gave us Jesus to claim victory over Satan. You deserve all of our love and praise.

In Jesus' name we pray,
Amen

1. As soon as Adam and Eve disobeyed God and sin entered the world, God told them that He would send a Rescuer to save them. What does that tell you about God and His character?

_____

_____

_____

_____

_____

_____

2. Every page of the Bible points to Jesus—even the pages in the Old Testament. How does that change how you view the Bible?

_____

_____

_____

_____

_____

_____

_____

3. Jesus was always the plan—the one and only plan. And the story of the whole Bible is the story about Jesus. How does that change the way you view the word "gospel"?

_____

_____

_____

_____

_____

_____

_____

BETTER THAN Eden

Adam and Eve disobeyed God and sin entered the world. This is why there is sin, pain, sickness, war, and death in our world today. All sin has consequences. This is also why we are sinners from the very beginning. As human beings, we come from Adam and Eve. But we also don't obey our parents perfectly. We aren't always nice, and sometimes, we find it hard to share our things or tell the truth. Deep down, we know that we are sinners.

But as we learned yesterday, as soon as sin entered the world, God told us that a Rescuer would come, which is good news! This is good news for us because, as sinners, we need a Savior that will pay the price for our sins so that we can live in God's presence again. The Promised Savior is Jesus, and He did come! After Adam and Eve sinned, it was thousands of years before Jesus came. A lot happened, and we read about it in the Old Testament in the Bible. There was a lot of sin and war and pain and death, but we see in the Bible that God always showed kindness and love and mercy to sinners. He wanted them to repent, which means to turn away from their sin and obey God. Some did, but many didn't.

IT WAS 100% CLEAR THAT THE PEOPLE ON EARTH NEEDED
A SAVIOR TO COME RESCUE THEM FROM THEIR SINS.

And Jesus, the Son of God, came quietly as a baby, and that is why we have the New Testament in the Bible and why we celebrate Christmas each year. He came exactly the way God told His people that He would come, from the tribe of Judah (Gen. 49:10), from the line of David (Isa. 9:6-7) by a virgin (Isa. 7:14), and in the town of Bethlehem (Mic. 5:2). Jesus lived a perfect life, and He could only do that because He is the Son of God. He was the true and better Adam. He completely obeyed God the Father where Adam did not. He did not sin, whereas Adam did. Instead, He took our place on the cross to pay the penalty for our sins. But three days later, He rose from the dead and went back to God the Father.

And today, we wait for Jesus to come back again just as He promised He would. But this time when He returns, it won't be as a baby. He will come as a powerful judge. He will create a new earth that will be even better than the Garden of Eden and His children will be able to live in His presence. It will be even better than Eden because there won't be temptations and there won't be any opportunity to sin, which demands death.

Look, God's dwelling is with humanity, and he will live with them. They will be his peoples, and God himself will be with them and will be their God. He will wipe away every tear from their eyes. Death will be no more; grief and crying, and pain will be no more, because the previous things have passed away.
REVELATIONS 21:3-4

Dear God,

Thank You for the good news of Jesus!
Thank You for the cross and for being
a loving and good God. We believe that
You will come back again, just as You
said you would. Help us live a life of
obedience to You while we wait.

In Jesus' name we pray,
Amen

1. Do you know that you're a sinner? As a sinner, what do you need?

2. Jesus came exactly the way the prophets in the Old Testament said He would come. When He came, that was the first Christmas. We are in a time of waiting for Him to come back. How will He come the second time?

3. When Jesus comes back, He isn't going to just remake the Garden of Eden. It's going to be even better. Why is the new earth going to be even better?

CAIN AND ABEL

Do you have a brother? Do you have a sister? The first siblings in the Bible were two brothers named Cain and Abel. Cain was the big brother of Abel. They were born after their parents, Adam and Eve, sinned and had to leave the Garden of Eden. This meant these two brothers grew up having to work really, really hard with their dad to grow food and take care of the animals. Cain's job was to take care of the garden. He worked the dirt so it would bring forth fruits and veggies. Abel was a shepherd, which meant he took care of the animals.

Back in those days, people would bring special gifts to God to show Him how much they loved Him. The Bible tells us what each brother brought:

In the course of time Cain presented some of the land's produce as an offering to the Lord. And Abel also presented an offering — some of the firstborn of his flock and their fat portions.
GENESIS 4:3-4

God knew that Cain did not give his very best to God, but his little brother, Abel, did. These gifts showed each of the brother's hearts — how much they loved God and if they even believed God was really God. Cain was jealous of his brother, even though he knew his brother brought the gifts that God asked for. Cain was so jealous and angry that he tricked his brother to go to a hidden field so he could secretly kill him — and he did! But people can't hide their sins from God. God knew right away what Cain did and punished him.

God called Abel righteous, which means free from the guilt of sin, because his gift showed that he believed in God. Even though Abel never saw God like his parents did in the Garden of Eden, he believed and that's called faith. Faith is believing in God even though you can't see Him with your eyes. And Abel brought the firstborn, fattest, and probably the purest animal he had. This was the best that Abel had.

We can learn a lot from Abel. We can learn to believe God even when we can't see Him with our eyes and to live the way God asks us to live as a gift to show our love and faith. But when we think about Abel, may we think about Jesus, who is the true and better Abel. You see, Jesus gives the better gift. He gives up His life as a gift for us. He doesn't sacrifice a spotless lamb like Abel did. No, Jesus was the spotless lamb because He lived a perfect, sinless life and gave up His life on the cross to take the punishment of our sins. Abel obeyed God in giving the right gift, and God said he was righteous because of his faith. Jesus obeyed God by being the ultimate gift and offers us His righteousness if we put our faith in Him. Between the two brothers, Abel was the hero in this story, but he wasn't perfect. But Abel reminds us that the Promised Savior, the perfect hero, is coming.

THIS PERFECT HERO IS JESUS, AND HE IS GOD'S BEST GIFT TO US.

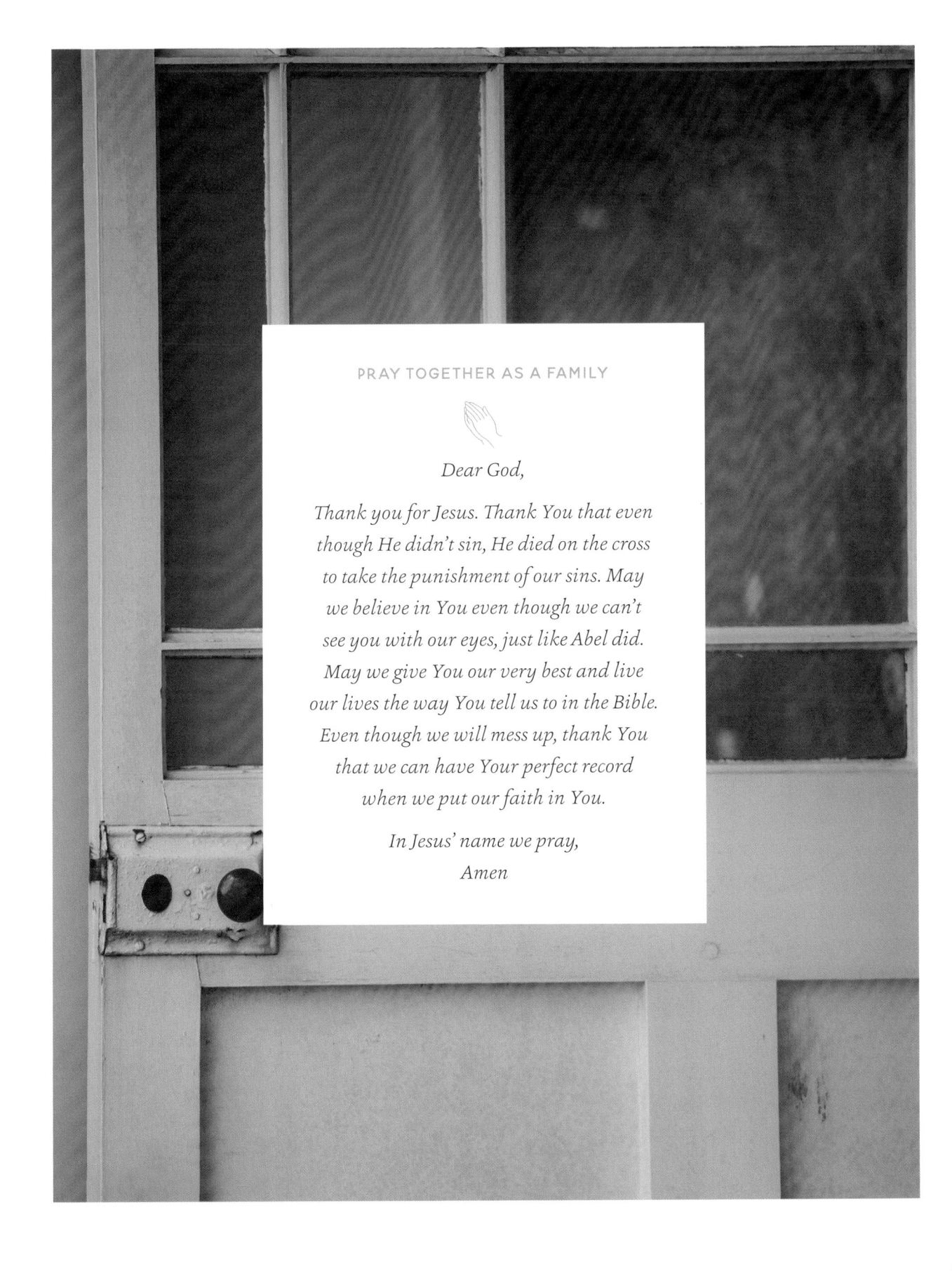

Dear God,

Thank you for Jesus. Thank You that even though He didn't sin, He died on the cross to take the punishment of our sins. May we believe in You even though we can't see you with our eyes, just like Abel did. May we give You our very best and live our lives the way You tell us to in the Bible. Even though we will mess up, thank You that we can have Your perfect record when we put our faith in You.

In Jesus' name we pray,
Amen

1. Why did God accept Abel's gift but not Cain's gift?

2. How is Jesus a true and better Abel?

3. What does it mean to be called righteous?
   How do we obtain righteousness today?

DOWN CAME The Rain

God is just, which means that He is always fair. He never over punishes and He never under punishes. So Cain was cursed for killing his little brother, Abel. He was sent away from God's presence, and he would wander around with no direction. But God showed Cain mercy. Sadly, his grandson's grandson's son (did you get that?), whose name was Lamech, was sinful, too. He ended up killing another human, which just showed that sin was spreading like a wildfire and causing a lot of pain and death in the world. People were forgetting about God and choosing to only think about themselves. The Bible tells us exactly what God thought about how the world was:

When the Lord saw that human wickedness was widespread on the earth and that every inclination of the human mind was nothing but evil all the time, the Lord regretted that he had made man on the earth, and he was deeply grieved.
GENESIS 6:5-6

God's heart was heavy, but He was not surprised – He had a plan. You see, before it got to this point, God had given Adam another son named Seth. And Seth also had sons who had sons. And down Seth's family line, there was a Lamech, too. But this Lamech had a son named Noah, and God was going to bring the Promised Savior from this family tree. Even though everyone else in the world was wicked and evil, Noah was God's friend. The Bible says Noah was a "righteous man and walked with God" (Gen. 6:9). So God told Noah that He was going to give the world a do-over. He was going to drown away all of the wickedness with a flood. But because God is just, He wouldn't wash Noah away because Noah was righteous. God is faithful too, which means He always does what He says He will do.

So God gave Noah all of the instructions to build a huge boat, called an ark. Even though God told Noah exactly how to build this ark, Noah had to trust and obey God and actually build the ark. And Noah had to have faith to believe in God even though he couldn't see Him. He believed what God said and built a boat even though he lived nowhere near the ocean. Then God brought two of every sort of animal so that they could start over, too. And God protected them in the ark while the rain poured down. After 370 days on the ark, the earth dried up enough for Noah to leave the ark. As soon as he did, he built an altar to God to show his gratitude for remembering him and his family. God was very happy and made a covenant with Noah, which is a promise that can never be broken. He promised to never wash everything away again, and He told Noah that a rainbow would be a reminder for people of this promise. Then God gave Noah the same command He gave to Adam: have kids and enjoy the earth!

Now, Noah was the hero in this story, but he wasn't perfect. Soon after this promise, the Bible said Noah drank too much wine, which wasn't good because that made him not think clearly. And when that happens, people can't live the way God wants them to live. But this story reminds us of the perfect hero that will come and that hero is Jesus. Instead of drinking wine, Jesus will drink the cup of God's wrath, which is the judgment that our sins deserve. He will save us, not from a flood, but from our sins and an eternity (which means forever) away from God.

THE WOODEN ARK REMINDS US OF THE WOODEN CROSS THAT JESUS WOULD BEAR. IT IS A SYMBOL OF GRACE, WHICH IS GETTING SOMETHING YOU DON'T DESERVE, AND A REFUGE, WHICH IS SAFETY FROM GOD'S RIGHTFUL JUDGMENT.

PRAY TOGETHER AS A FAMILY

Dear God,

Thank You for being just and for always being fair. Thank You for being faithful and always doing what You say you will do. Thank You for that unbreakable promise that You made with Noah to never flood the earth again. But more than that, thank You for Jesus, the Promised Savior. Thank You that He came to save us not from a flood, but from our sins, which deserves forever punishment away from You. Jesus is our ark where we can find safety.

In Jesus' name we pray,
Amen

1. If God drowned every single person and every single animal from the earth, He wouldn't have kept His promise that the Rescuer would come from Adam and Eve's family tree. What does that tell you about God, His character, and His plan?

2. Noah had to have faith in God. He had to believe what God said (rain was coming) and to obey (build the ark). Has there ever been a time when you had to have faith?

3. Jesus is like the ark. He is our safe place and provides a way out from the flood of divine judgment. But like Noah, we are called to trust and obey God. How can you trust and obey God today?

A
RESCUE STORY

BETTER THAN
Eden

CAIN AND ABEL

DOWN CAME
CAME
The Rain

Everywhere on Earth

After the flood, Noah and his sons did what God said to do. They grew their family. But God also told them to fill the earth (Gen. 9:1), which meant they had to spread out. You see, God wanted the whole earth to be filled with His image bearers (humans) that would worship Him. But this is where they disobeyed. The number of people on earth grew, but they purposefully stayed in one area. They built a city and tried to make a tower to reach heaven because they wanted to make a name for themselves and didn't want to be "scattered throughout the earth" (Gen. 11:4). They were working hard to do exactly the opposite of what God told them to do. Does it turn out well when you do the opposite of what your parents tell you to do?

God, out of his love for people, stepped in. In order to stop people from getting into more trouble, God forced them to spread out by creating different languages so it made it hard for them to talk to each other. Do you think you could build a huge tower with people that spoke French or Chinese or Arabic? It's hard to figure out who is doing what when you can't communicate! This was called the Tower of Babel. They didn't obey God to fill the earth, but we serve a mighty God that has a plan that cannot be stopped. His plans don't depend on our obedience, and that's a good thing!

> *Therefore it is called Babylon, for there the Lord confused the language of the all the earth, and from there the Lord scattered them throughout the earth.*
> GENESIS 11:9

But what was the big deal? Weren't they getting along and working together nicely to build this tower? You see, the real issue here was pride, and God hates pride (Prov. 8:13). When it comes to sin, it's usually the heart behind the actual act that is the biggest problem. And what's often found at the heart of all sin is pride.

PRIDE IS BASICALLY YOUR HEART SCREAMING, "MOVE OVER, GOD! I AM IN CHARGE, AND I AM GOING TO DO WHAT I WANT TO DO!"

Have you ever felt that way? What we are really saying is that we love ourselves more than God. So that was the real issue at the Tower of Babel. The people had turned away from God in their pride, and the tower was like a trophy for other people to see. They wanted people to admire them instead of God.

All of this happened less than 100 years after the flood! It doesn't take long for the human heart to rebel against God. And as we said, all sin has consequences and that's called judgment. In the flood, the judgment came in the form of total destruction of the world. In this story, judgment is the scattering of the people. But this was actually God's common grace toward people. He was protecting them. God knew that if the people stayed with one language, they would end up with an evil leader that would have nothing to restrain his wickedness. The division of people and talents and resources was protection against themselves.

But soon, the promised Rescuer will come and gather His people "from the ends of the earth to the ends of the heaven" (Mark 13:27). He will deliver the final judgment and create a new heaven and a new earth with no sin. He will be the good King that rules over a unified kingdom! But until then, we can trust that God is in control of all of the big things in this world, like gravity and the universe. But He's also aware of the details, too. He knows every motive in your heart and mine! So we have to remember that we can't make a tower high enough to reach God in heaven. We can't be God! Plus, God's plan is better: the Son of God, Jesus, will come down from heaven to make a way back to Him.

PRAY TOGETHER AS A FAMILY

Dear God,

Thank You for being in control of the whole wide world. Thank You for also knowing the things in our hearts. We learned from this story that Your plan will happen because You are God and You are in control – Your plan does not depend on our perfect obedience. Even though people were forced to scatter across the earth, You will send the Rescuer to gather Your people again. May we say "no" to pride and "yes" to obedience to You. We want You to get all of the glory.

In Jesus' name we pray,
Amen

1. Before the Tower of Babel, everyone spoke the same language. After God came down, everyone spoke different languages. Why did God do that?

_____

_____

_____

_____

_____

2. Sometimes God does things that might seem confusing, but He knows everything and does it out of love for His people. How was spreading people out an act of love?

_____

_____

_____

_____

_____

_____

_____

3. God holds the whole universe in His hands. Yet, He knows every detail of your heart and life. How does that make you feel?

_____

_____

_____

_____

_____

_____

_____

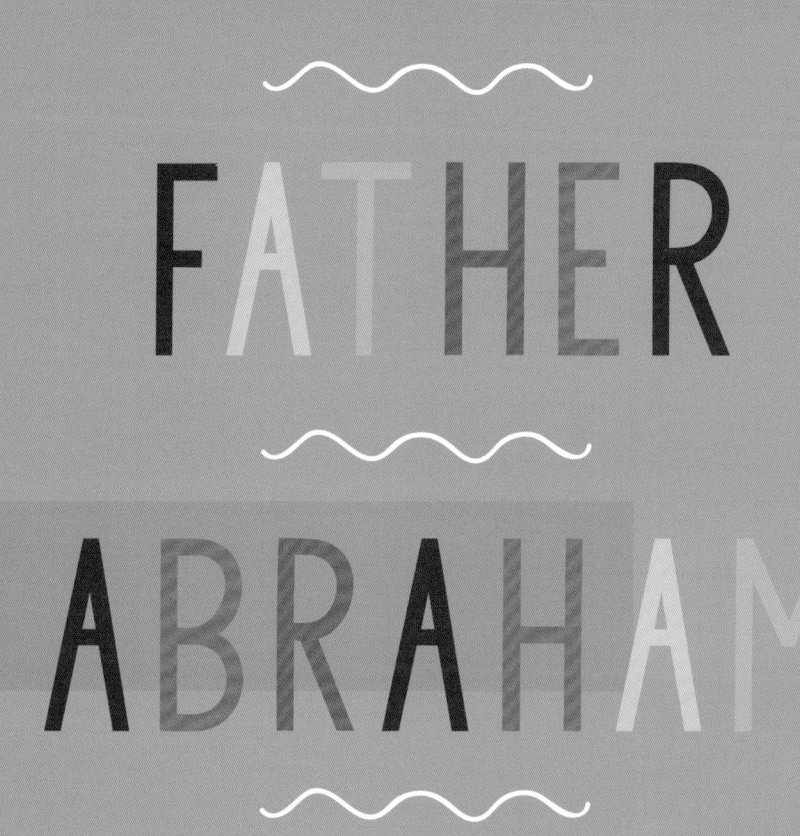

FATHER
ABRAHAM

After the Tower of Babel, only one person is named along with his descendants. His name is Peleg, which means divided. Peleg's grandson's grandson's name was Terah, and Terah had three sons named Abram, Nahor, and Haran. It had been over 1,000 years since the Promised Savior was first mentioned in Genesis 3:15, and by the time Terah was born, people were finding it hard to wait for Him. In fact, the Bible says Terah and his neighbors worshiped other gods (Josh. 24:2). They made up their own gods called idols. If we love anything or anyone more than we love God, that thing or person is an idol. Human hearts want to make idols all the time, so that's why we have to be on guard! God chose Terah's son, Abram, to carry out His grand plan. The Bible doesn't say that Abram was looking for God at the time; instead, it says that God called Abram.

Go from your land, your relatives, and your father's house to the land that I will show you. I will make you into a great nation, I will bless you, I will make your name great, and you will be a blessing. I will bless those who bless you. I will curse anyone who treats you with contempt, and all the peoples on the earth will be blessed through you.

GENESIS 12:1-3

Do you notice how God said, "I will" five times? God was saying that He was going to carry out the plan through Abram. In fact, this is called the Abrahamic covenant, which we know, is a promise that God will never break. But Abram had to obey and have faith. You see, God told Abram to leave the place he called home, which happened to be a cool city. And he had to believe in God and His promise, which meant he had to have faith. Now, it might seem like an easy promise to believe in. God said his family tree would be so big that you wouldn't even be able to count the people in it, kind of like how you can't really count the number of stars in the sky (Gen. 15:5). But here's what you may not know. Abram and his wife, Sarai, were already old, and Sarai's body couldn't have babies. So God's rescue plan had some humanly impossible missions. How could Abram have a big family tree when he and his wife couldn't even have kids? Now it makes more sense why Abram had to have faith in God and His grand plan!

But Abram did believe and he also obeyed and left his home and everything that was familiar to him. For 24 years, Abram lived and "called upon the name of the Lord" (Gen. 12:8), and Sarai still didn't have a baby. But when Abram was 99 years old, God affirmed his promise again and changed his name to Abraham, which means father of many nations, and Sarai became Sarah. God told Abraham that Sarah would have a son the following year when he would be 100 years old and Sarah would be 90 years old. You know what happened, right? They had a son right when God said they would, and his name was Isaac!

So how does all of this point to Jesus? You see, God promised to make Abraham's family a great and special nation, called Israel. And he did. Isaac had a son named Jacob, and Jacob had 12 sons that became the 12 tribes of Israel. And the reason God made this promise and built Abraham's

family tree was Jesus. It is through Jesus that God would fulfill the promise that He gave Abraham in the very beginning in Genesis 12:3 – that all the families of the earth will be blessed, not just Israel, which is good news for you and me! Abraham obeyed God and left his familiar home to follow God's plan; Jesus would leave his heavenly home and live a life of perfect obedience to fulfill God's plan. Abraham showed us what saving faith looks like when he believed God would do the impossible; Jesus did what was impossible for us to do on our own and is the One we put our faith in today.

PRAY TOGETHER AS A FAMILY

Dear God,

Thank You for Your perfect plan. Help us guard our hearts against loving anything or anyone more than You. Help us to believe in all of the promises that You give us in Your Word. Thank You, Jesus, for willingly leaving Your heavenly home to do what we could not do. You lived a perfect life without sin and died on the cross to pay the penalty for our sins. Thank You that we can put our faith in You and be a part of Your family.

In Jesus' name we pray,
Amen

1. An idol is anything or anyone in your heart that you love more than God. Can you name any idols in your heart? Confess them to God in prayer.

_____

_____

_____

_____

_____

_____

2. God chooses to use particular people, and it often doesn't make sense why. And usually, God calls them to impossible missions that they cannot do without Him. Why do you think God works in this way?

_____

_____

_____

_____

_____

_____

3. God knew from the beginning that all families would be blessed through the work of Jesus. How does this story turn our hearts to Jesus and cause us to worship Him?

_____

_____

_____

_____

_____

GIVE
YOUR ONLY
SON

Like we said yesterday, Abraham and Sarah did have a son, and they named him Isaac. But Abraham had another son before Isaac. You see, after God first talked to Abraham about His grand plan about a big family, 10 years went by with no baby. As you can imagine, Abraham's wife, Sarah, was growing a bit impatient. She decided to take matters into her own hands to make Abraham have a child. She gave her personal servant, Hagar, to Abraham, and they had a son named Ishmael. But as we learned, God doesn't change His plans. Ishmael wasn't the promised son that God was going to use in His covenant with Abraham. God's plan was for Abraham and Sarah to have a son, and 13 years later, they did! At the very time God said, Sarah's body miraculously grew a baby—Isaac. But when Isaac was 13 years old, God told Abraham to do something really confusing:

"Take your son," he said, "your only son Isaac, whom you love, go to the land of Moriah, and offer him there as a burnt offering on one of the mountains I will tell you about."
GENESIS 22:2

You can imagine how confused Abraham must have been. God's promise to grow Abraham's family tree was supposed to happen through Isaac, their miracle baby. God told Abraham this clearly, "through Isaac shall your offspring be named" (Gen. 21:12). But now, God was telling Abraham to give Isaac back to Him. Do you know what Abraham did? He got up early the next morning (Gen. 22:3), cut the wood himself for the sacrifice (Gen. 22:3), and started the two-day journey to the land of Moriah with Isaac. On the way there, Isaac pointed out the obvious when he asked, "Where's the lamb to be sacrificed?" Abraham replied, "God will provide for himself the lamb for a burnt offering" (Gen. 22:8). They got to the mountain, and Abraham built the altar and tied his son, Isaac, to the wood. The Bible says Abraham even "reached out his hand and took the knife to slaughter his son" (Gen. 22:10). But, wait! At the very last moment, an angel of the Lord from heaven told him to stop. You see, God did provide the lamb. Abraham noticed a "ram caught in a thicket by its horns" nearby (Gen. 22:13).

You see, no matter how confusing God's request was, Abraham knew God would keep His promise. In fact, before he and Isaac even went up the mountain, Abraham told the servants that came with them that they would be back (Gen. 22:6). Abraham believed that God would either provide a substitute offering for Isaac or would raise Isaac from the dead in order to keep His promise. Even though Abraham was imperfect, he still modeled saving faith (Gen. 15:6). When we believe God and His promises and obey Him, we are counted as righteous, which means we are in right relationship with God.

This story clearly points us to Jesus. Jesus is the true and better Isaac. Jesus, God's only son, was sacrificed to pay the price for our sins. Just like Isaac didn't wrestle with his dad when he was tied to the wood, Jesus doesn't resist the Father's will, which included the wooden cross. Jesus was the ram, the substitute offering provided by God that died on the cross to pay the penalty for our sins. Jesus' royal lineage goes all the way back to this Abrahamic covenant, and He is the Promised One, the truly miraculous baby.

WHEN WE BELIEVE GOD AND HIS PROMISES AND OBEY HIM, WE ARE COUNTED AS RIGHTEOUS, WHICH MEANS WE ARE IN RIGHT RELATIONSHIP WITH GOD.

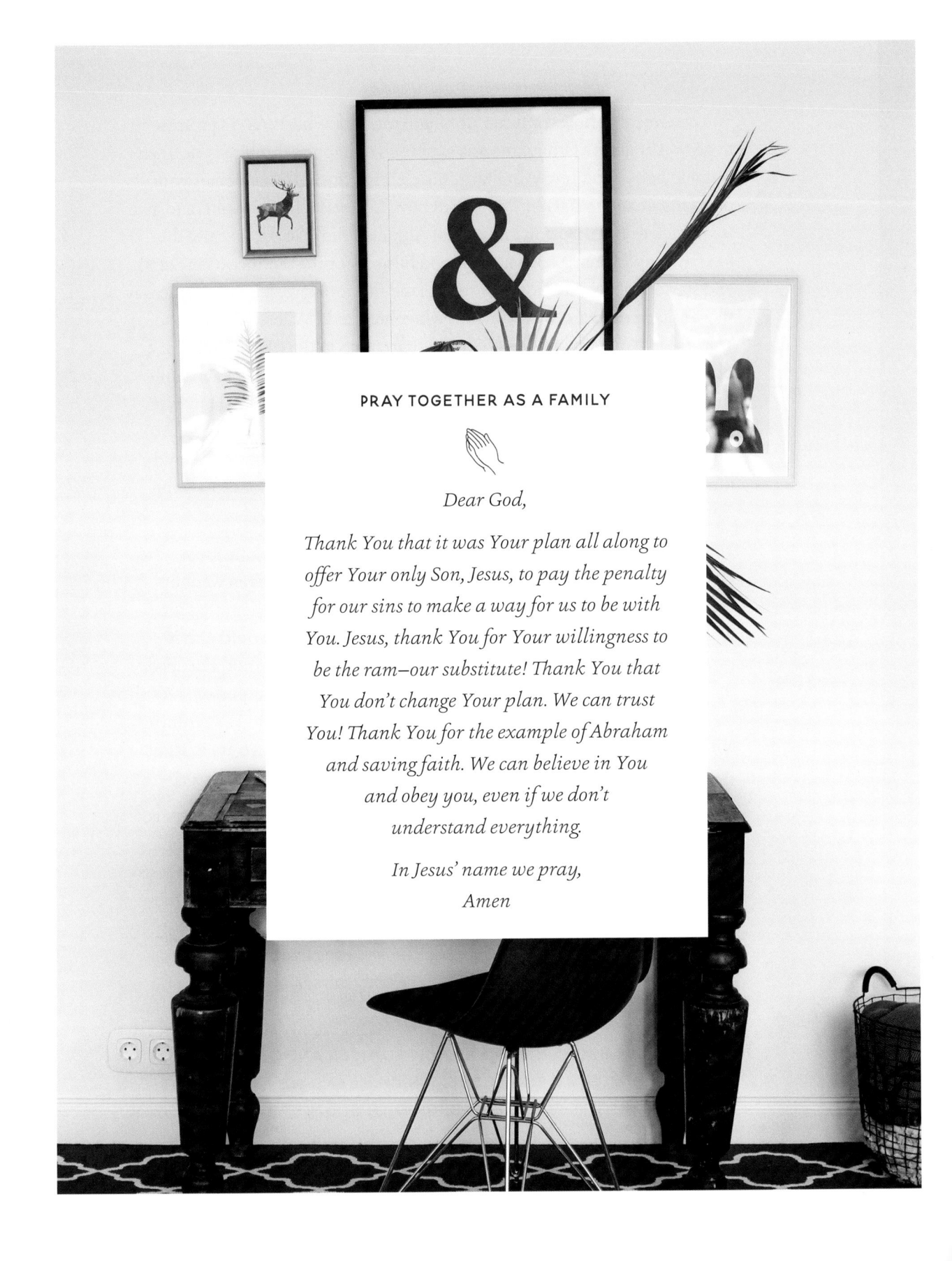

PRAY TOGETHER AS A FAMILY

Dear God,

Thank You that it was Your plan all along to offer Your only Son, Jesus, to pay the penalty for our sins to make a way for us to be with You. Jesus, thank You for Your willingness to be the ram—our substitute! Thank You that You don't change Your plan. We can trust You! Thank You for the example of Abraham and saving faith. We can believe in You and obey you, even if we don't understand everything.

In Jesus' name we pray,
Amen

1. Abraham is an example of saving faith. What is saving faith?

_____

_____

_____

_____

_____

_____

2. Why do you think God asked Abraham to give Him his son, Isaac?

_____

_____

_____

_____

_____

_____

_____

3. How does this story of Abraham and Isaac show us what will happen later with Jesus?

_____

_____

_____

_____

_____

_____

_____

_____

REFLECTION QUESTIONS

Heel-Catcher
TO
GOD'S FIGHTER

We read how Abraham didn't hold tightly and say "no" to God when He asked him for his only son, Isaac (Gen. 22:12). Abraham's response actually showed his love and fear of God. It may seem like a strange thing for God to have asked that of Abraham, but we know that God would never ask us to do anything that He, Himself, would not do. In fact, more than Abraham, God did give up His only Son, Jesus, for us! So in the cross, we see God's great love for us!

Now Isaac grew up and married Rebekah. But like Sarah, Rebekah found that her body was not able to grow babies. After 20 years, the Bible tells us what Isaac did – he prayed. After Isaac prayed, Rebekah got pregnant. What a reminder that God is in control of carrying out His grand plan! God told her that she would have two babies, and the older would serve the younger. And He was right. Rebekah had twins, Esau and Jacob. And just like God chose Abraham and Isaac, He chose to carry out His covenant through Jacob, the younger brother, before he was even born. Jacob didn't do anything to earn this. In fact, his name actually means "heel-catcher," which is a Hebrew expression for "deceiver". Jacob was very sly! Instead of trusting in God's plan, Jacob took advantage of his older brother at a moment of weakness (Gen 25:31) and took his birthright, which legally made Jacob the firstborn. But when Isaac was old and blind, he wanted to pass on the family blessing to Esau. He favored Esau and wanted to stick to the cultural norm of passing things on to the firstborn son. But Jacob tricked Isaac and pretended to be Esau and got the family blessing.

ISAAC TREMBLED BECAUSE HE KNEW WHY THIS HAPPENED. IT HAPPENED BECAUSE GOD IS SOVEREIGN, WHICH MEANS HE IS IN TOTAL CONTROL OF HIS PLAN AND DOES EVERYTHING ACCORDING TO HIS PLAN.

As you can imagine, Esau hated Jacob. Actually, Jacob had to move away to a place called Haran because Esau wanted to kill him. On his way there, Jacob had a dream and God told Jacob his family tree will have the Promised Savior! Jacob lived there for 20 years and had 11 sons, and from them, a nation would come. But then God told Jacob to go back to the land of Canaan where his brother was. Even though many years had passed, Jacob was scared to face his brother! But instead of praying and trusting in God, Jacob relied on himself and schemed. He tried to butter Esau up by sending a lot of gifts. But the night before Jacob was to meet Esau, something strange happened. Jacob wrestled with a "man" all night. This man was actually the Son of God! Jacob said, "I have seen God face to face" (Gen. 32:30). Jacob didn't give up during the wrestling match, and at the very end, he asked God to bless him. Then God changed Jacob's name from "heel-catcher" to "God's fighter." Jacob would now be called Israel, and he would overcome with God. God left Jacob with a limp that would always remind him to rely on God and His plan instead of scheming.

Jesus would one day have a similar evening where He "wrestles" with God. The night before Jesus was appointed to face the wrath of God on the cross for our sins, He wrestled in prayer in the Garden of Gethsemane, but said "not my will, but yours, be done" (Luke 22:42). The night before Jacob was appointed to face the wrath of Esau, he wrestled and asked for God to bless him and God did. And Jacob never did face Esau's wrath. Esau ran to Jacob with hugs and kisses. But Jesus did drink the cup of God's wrath on the cross, which was the rightful punishment we deserved. Jacob's hip was wounded to remind him of God's divine grace; Jesus would be wounded unto death, and the cross is God's abundant grace toward us.

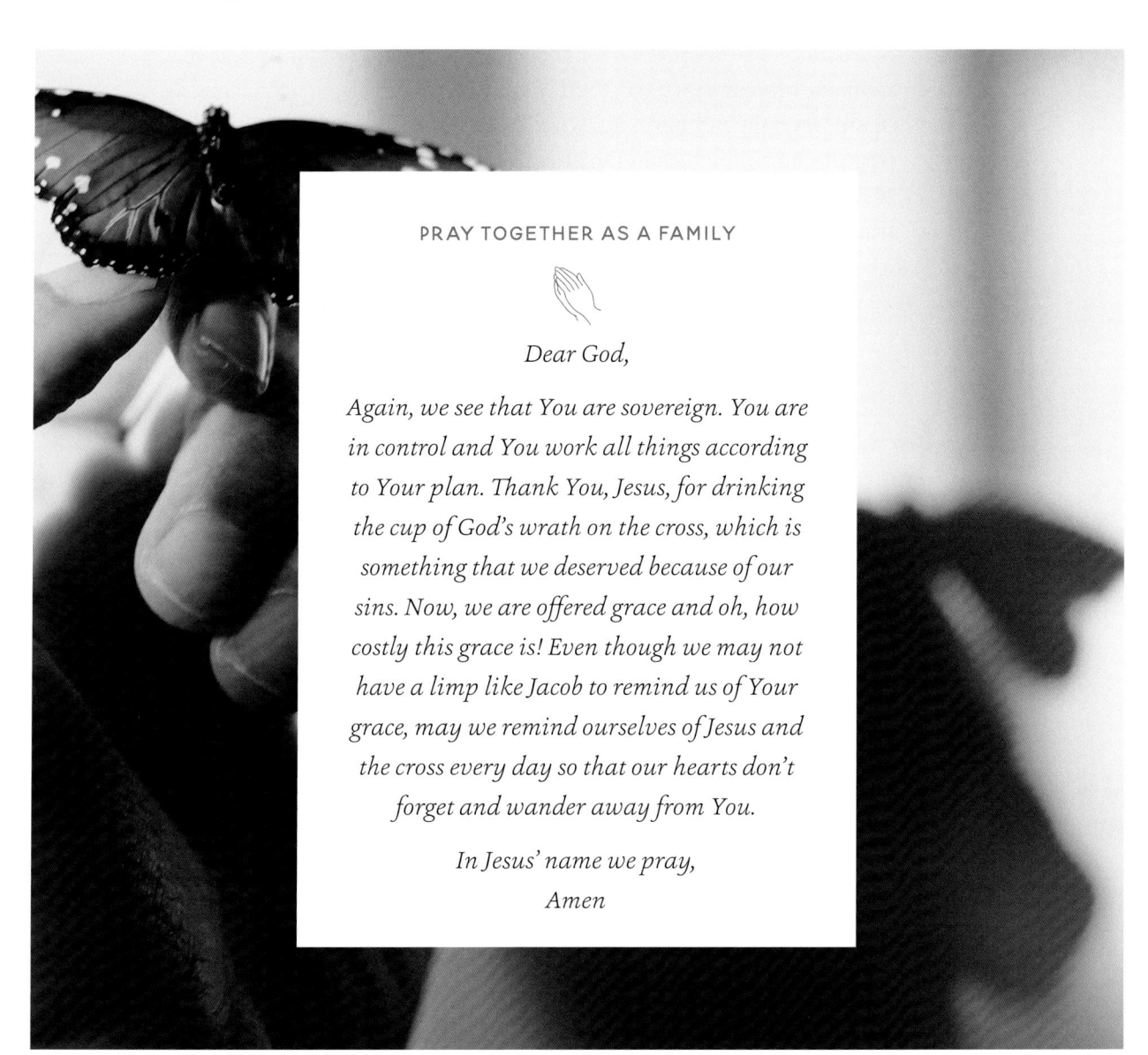

PRAY TOGETHER AS A FAMILY

Dear God,

Again, we see that You are sovereign. You are in control and You work all things according to Your plan. Thank You, Jesus, for drinking the cup of God's wrath on the cross, which is something that we deserved because of our sins. Now, we are offered grace and oh, how costly this grace is! Even though we may not have a limp like Jacob to remind us of Your grace, may we remind ourselves of Jesus and the cross every day so that our hearts don't forget and wander away from You.

In Jesus' name we pray,
Amen

1. Again, we see that God does things His way. Before the twins were born, He chose the younger to receive the covenant promise. Why do you think God did that?

_____

_____

_____

_____

_____

2. Jacob was often deceiving. Whenever there was a problem, he schemed to get his way. What does God want us to do instead?

_____

_____

_____

_____

_____

_____

3. We can also have times when we wrestle with God and His plan. In those seasons, how can we look to Jesus as our example?

_____

_____

_____

_____

_____

_____

Everywhere on Earth

~~~

FATHER

~~~

ABRAHAM

~~~

GIVE YOUR ONLY SON

Heel-Catcher
↳ TO ↲
GOD'S FIGHTER

Israel's FAVORITE SON

After a while, Jacob (or Israel, which was his new name from God) settled in the land of Canaan, which was the land that God promised to give Abraham and his family. He now had 12 sons, and they would later make up the whole nation of Israel. But of his 12 sons, Jacob favored Joseph and made him a special "robe of many colors" (Gen. 37:3). The robe was a symbol. Jacob was basically declaring that Joseph would be the future leader of the family even though he wasn't the firstborn son (he was actually number 11!). As you can imagine, Joseph's brothers did not like that one bit! In fact, they "hated him" (Gen. 37:4). It didn't help that Joseph told them about special dreams that he had which predicted that Joseph would rule over his brothers one day! Later, some of the brothers talked about killing Joseph. Don't worry. They didn't kill their brother, but they did steal his special robe and threw him into a pit! Then Judah, one of the brothers, suggested selling him to foreigners, as if he were a slave, to make money! After they got rid of Joseph, the brothers covered his tunic in goat's blood and took it to their dad and made him think that a fierce animal gobbled up his favorite son.

But God is in control, remember? A lot happened after Joseph was sold into slavery, but it was clear that God was with Joseph. God gave him favor and made him successful. After 13 years, Joseph went from slave to second-in-command in Egypt (Gen. 41:42). You see, God was going to bring a harsh famine to Egypt, but he gave Pharaoh a warning in a few confusing dreams. God told Joseph what those dreams meant so that he could tell Pharaoh and find favor. So it was God that put Joseph in a powerful position in Pharaoh's office to save His covenant family and the nation of Israel from a global famine. And we see that Joseph's dreams from his teenage years did come true. His brothers ended up bowing down to him when they came to him in Egypt for food. When the brothers realized that Joseph was alive and a powerful man, they were afraid that he would want to have revenge on them. But this is what Joseph said:

> *Don't be afraid. Am I in the place of God? You planned evil against me; God planned it for good to bring about the present result – the survival of many people. Therefore don't be afraid. I will take care of you and your children.*
> GENESIS 50:19-21

Joseph teaches us to trust in God even when things are going bad for us, to work hard at whatever God puts before us, to forgive those who wrong us, and to do good, always. Joseph is a "type" of Christ, which just means he is a picture of Jesus. Before Joseph was sold into slavery, he was a shepherd of his dad's sheep. Jesus is the Shepherd of His people. Joseph was dearly loved by his dad; Jesus was His Father's only beloved son. Joseph was hated by his brothers and they conspired to kill him; Jesus was hated by His Jewish brothers and they conspired to kill Him. In Pharaoh's house, Joseph was tempted, falsely accused, and then bound in chains in prison. Jesus was tempted in the wilderness, falsely accused by chief priests, and bound and taken to Pilate, the governor.

But Jesus is the true and better Joseph. Joseph was sold into slavery, forced from beloved son to slave. Jesus willingly left His heavenly home to become a servant and die on the cross. Joseph saved his covenant family, the nation of Israel, from starvation and death. Jesus truly saves His people

from the penalty of sin, which is death. Joseph forgave his brothers for the wrong they did to him; Jesus makes a way for us to be forgiven for all of our sins. Joseph was elevated to Pharaoh's right hand and saw his brothers bow down to him; Jesus is at the Father's right hand, and soon, every knee will bow and every tongue will confess that Jesus is Lord (Rom. 14:11). Even though the Abrahamic covenant is carried out through Judah, and not Joseph, God used Joseph to preserve the family tree and to give a clear glimpse of the saving work that God would do through Jesus.

JESUS IS THE TRUE AND BETTER JOSEPH.

PRAY TOGETHER AS A FAMILY

Dear God,

Thank You for giving us a clear picture of Jesus in the Old Testament. Again, we can see so clearly that Jesus was always the plan. Thank You that you used Joseph to preserve the "seed" – the nation of Israel and the family line that would bring the Messiah, Jesus. May we, like Joseph, always trust You, do good, and forgive others. May we look to Jesus and the saving work He did on the cross.

In Jesus' name we pray,
Amen

1. A lot of things went wrong for Joseph, but he trusted in God's sovereignty. What do we learn about Joseph's character?

2. How is Joseph a "type" of Christ?

3. God used Joseph to protect His people from a global famine. God preserved His people because of His promise. We can trust that He will do what He says! How does this encourage us right now in our waiting for Jesus to come back a second time?

JUST GO!

Joseph's family settled in Egypt, and God's promise that Abraham's family would grow actually happened. After 400 years, they were more the size of a nation! But there was a new king over Egypt. He didn't know about Joseph, and all he could see was that the Israelites were growing in number and that intimidated him. In order to control their growth, the Egyptians made the Israelites become their slaves and even ordered that every male Israelite baby be killed! But this didn't catch God by surprise. He was going to make a way for His people. At this time, a Hebrew baby boy named Moses was born, and his mother made a way for him to be found by Pharaoh's daughter. This princess protected him from death, adopted him, and raised him as if he were a noble Egyptian. But Moses never forgot that he was an Israelite, and when he was older, he killed an Egyptian in order to protect a Hebrew slave. When word got around, Moses feared for his life and fled to Midian.

Forty years passed, and Moses lived a normal life in Midian. He was a shepherd, was married, and started a family. But the Israelites were still enslaved in Egypt, and they cried out to God for help. God heard them and saw them, and He remembered His promise. So God called out to Moses through a burning bush — yes, a bush that was on fire but the leaves and branches didn't burn up! God told Moses His plan: Moses was going to go back to Egypt to free the Israelites. God even told Moses how He would deliver them to a good land "flowing with milk and honey" (Exodus 3:8, 17). Despite some initial hesitation, Moses did end up trusting and obeying.

Pharaoh's heart was hard, and he was stubborn. God stretched out his hand and struck Egypt with plagues. The water turned to blood. There was infestation of frogs, then gnats, and then flies. All of the Egyptians' livestock died. There were boils on the Egyptians' bodies. There was a severe hail storm. Then there was another invasion, but this time of locusts. There was complete darkness for three days. And finally came the death of every firstborn. For the final plague, the Israelites were instructed to sacrifice a young, male lamb without blemish, at twilight (around 3PM) and to sprinkle its blood around their doorway. This would be a sign for the angel of death to pass over the house and save the firstborns from death. God gave them specific instructions for this particular meal, and even told them to be dressed in a way that they could leave at a moment's notice. At midnight, the plague struck and all of the Egyptian families cried out at the death of their firstborns. Pharaoh immediately ordered the Israelites to leave Egypt, and the Israelites walked out of the land of slavery and toward the land promised to them in the Abrahamic covenant.

THIS IS CALLED THE EXODUS.

The Israelites were instructed to prepare this Passover meal every year as a memorial – a feast to not forget how God had delivered them from Egypt. The Passover taught the Israelites that in order to be delivered from judgment, death was needed, but this death could only be the death of an innocent substitute. This was why they did animal sacrifices. But this points us to the true and better Passover Lamb. Jesus is the spotless lamb of God that was sacrificed to save us from death (John 1:29). He was the innocent substitute that was killed at twilight on the cross to deliver us from divine judgment. Before Jesus died, He celebrated His last Passover meal with His disciples. It was then that He introduced communion (Luke 22:14). You see, after Jesus ate the lamb at the last Passover meal, He was going to be the lamb. Now He was bringing a new command, communion or the Lord's supper, which believers partake in today. Communion is a symbol of Christ's body given to His people and the New Covenant in His blood. Communion is done to remember Jesus and His work on the cross, and we are commanded to do it until He returns.

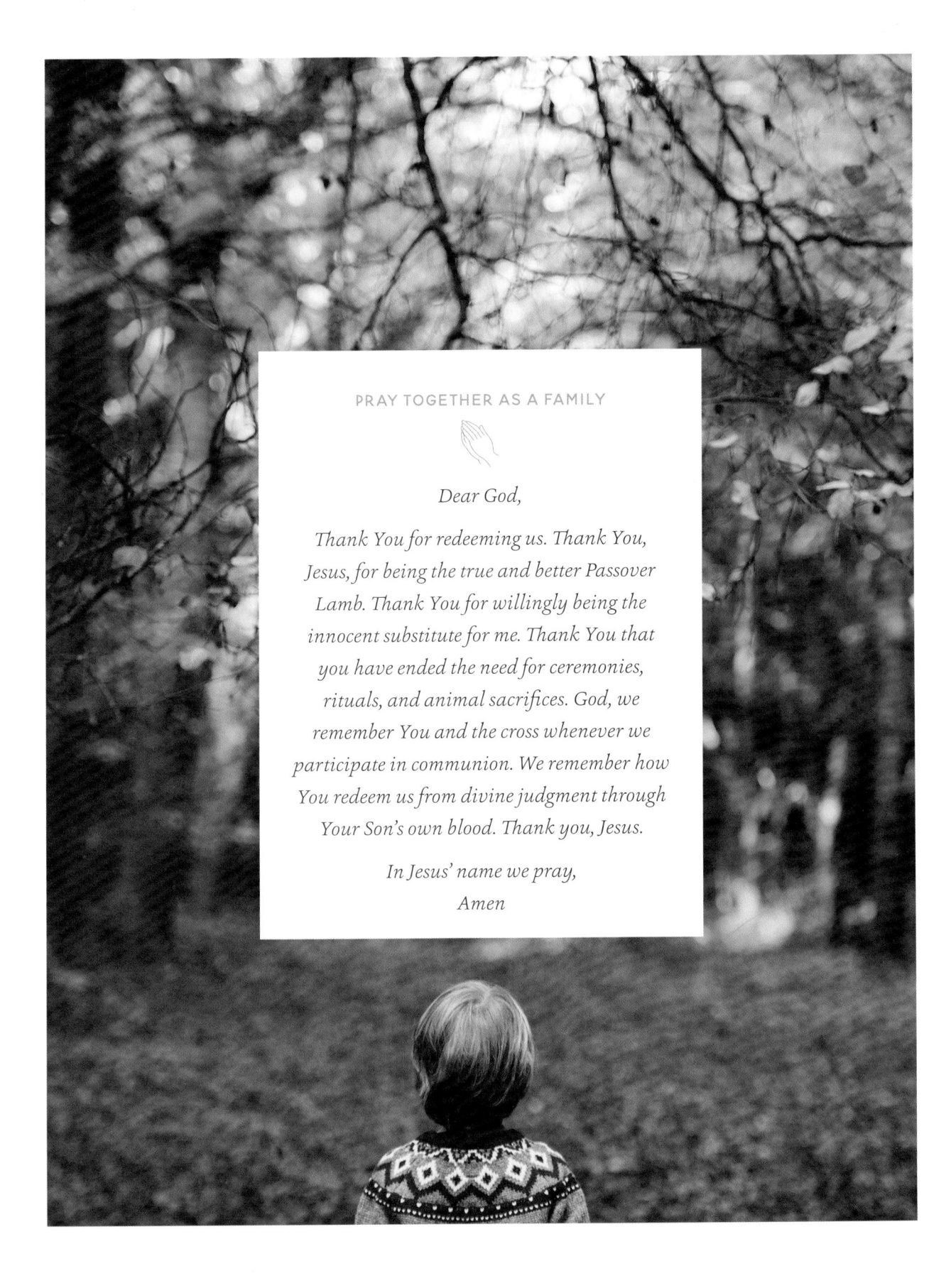

PRAY TOGETHER AS A FAMILY

Dear God,

Thank You for redeeming us. Thank You, Jesus, for being the true and better Passover Lamb. Thank You for willingly being the innocent substitute for me. Thank You that you have ended the need for ceremonies, rituals, and animal sacrifices. God, we remember You and the cross whenever we participate in communion. We remember how You redeem us from divine judgment through Your Son's own blood. Thank you, Jesus.

In Jesus' name we pray,
Amen

1. God's people were enslaved in Egypt for hundreds of years, but we read in Genesis 12 that God told Abraham that this would happen and He had a plan to rescue them. He makes bitter things sweet. Has there ever been a time when God used something hard in your life and later used it for your good and His glory?

2. God chose Moses even though He knew Moses' weaknesses (he wasn't a strong public speaker). When God calls us to do something hard, how should we respond?

3. The Passover in the Old Testament is very important. How is Jesus the true and better Passover Lamb?

KEEP THE Commandments

The Israelites were on their way to the Promised Land, but God led them "toward the Red Sea along the road of the wilderness." (Exod. 13:18). God guided them. He was a pillar of cloud in the day and a pillar of fire in the night for them to follow (Exod. 14:21). Sounds out of this world, right? God was going to show His divine power in many ways throughout this journey. But not long after the Israelites left, Pharaoh changed his mind and wanted them back. But God protected His people by splitting the Red Sea and the Israelites walked across on dry ground while the Egyptians were swallowed up by the waters.

After celebrating this mighty work of God, the Israelites were on their way to Mount Sinai. Three days later, they started to grumble because they were thirsty. How did God respond? He used Moses to throw a log into the water to make it sweet (Exod. 15:25). Weeks went by and their bellies grumbled, and they thought, "Remember all of the good food we had in Egypt? God brought us out here to die!" How quickly they forgot all that God had done! But do you know how God responded? He rained down bread (manna) every single day for them. And He gave them meat, too. Our God always provides! They finally made it to Mt. Sinai, and something big happened. God invited them into a covenant. He told them:

Now if you will carefully listen to me and keep my covenant, you will be my own possession out of all the peoples, although the whole earth is mine,

EXODUS 19:5

But did you catch that? God said if they obeyed then they would be set apart for His purposes. Moses led them to the foot of the mountain, and they could see a cloud covering the top of the mountain that symbolized God's presence. God was making it clear that He was giving Moses the commandments for the people to obey as part of the Mosaic covenant. These are the ten commandments. You may think it's a list of rules that you have to follow to earn God's favor and be saved, but it's not. If you look at the commandments, you'll see that the first half deals with people's relationship to God and the second half deals with people's relationship to each other. God, out of love, was telling them how life works best. When God told them to love Him most, not let idols crowd their hearts, not misuse His name, rest on the Sabbath, respect their parents, don't murder, steal, lie, or envy others, He was telling them their obedience to these things was a response to the faith they had in God. What God was after was love—a love that is expressed by obedience. It is love that hits the mark on all of these commandments.

And the Israelites eagerly agreed (Exod. 24:3). But as you'll see, they don't obey God perfectly. Not too long after this, the Israelites look to man-made gods to lead them. God knew they couldn't obey the law perfectly, but it was supposed to teach the Israelites about God's holiness and their

sinfulness. The law teaches us the same. We need divine grace that only Jesus can give. This is how the ten commandments point us to Jesus. You see, we are not so different from the Israelites. Just like they were on a journey from Egypt to the Promised Land, we are on a journey, too. Our journey is the time in between Jesus' resurrection and His second coming. We are waiting for Jesus to come back. The ten commandments show us that God is holy, we are sinful, and we need Jesus. But we, like the Israelites, are called to obey God's commands out of love for Him. We, like the Israelites, are called to live in such a way that would show the world about our God. As believers, we have the Holy Spirit inside of us that helps us to obey. We will never obey perfectly, but that's okay because we have Jesus who obeyed completely and perfectly in our place.

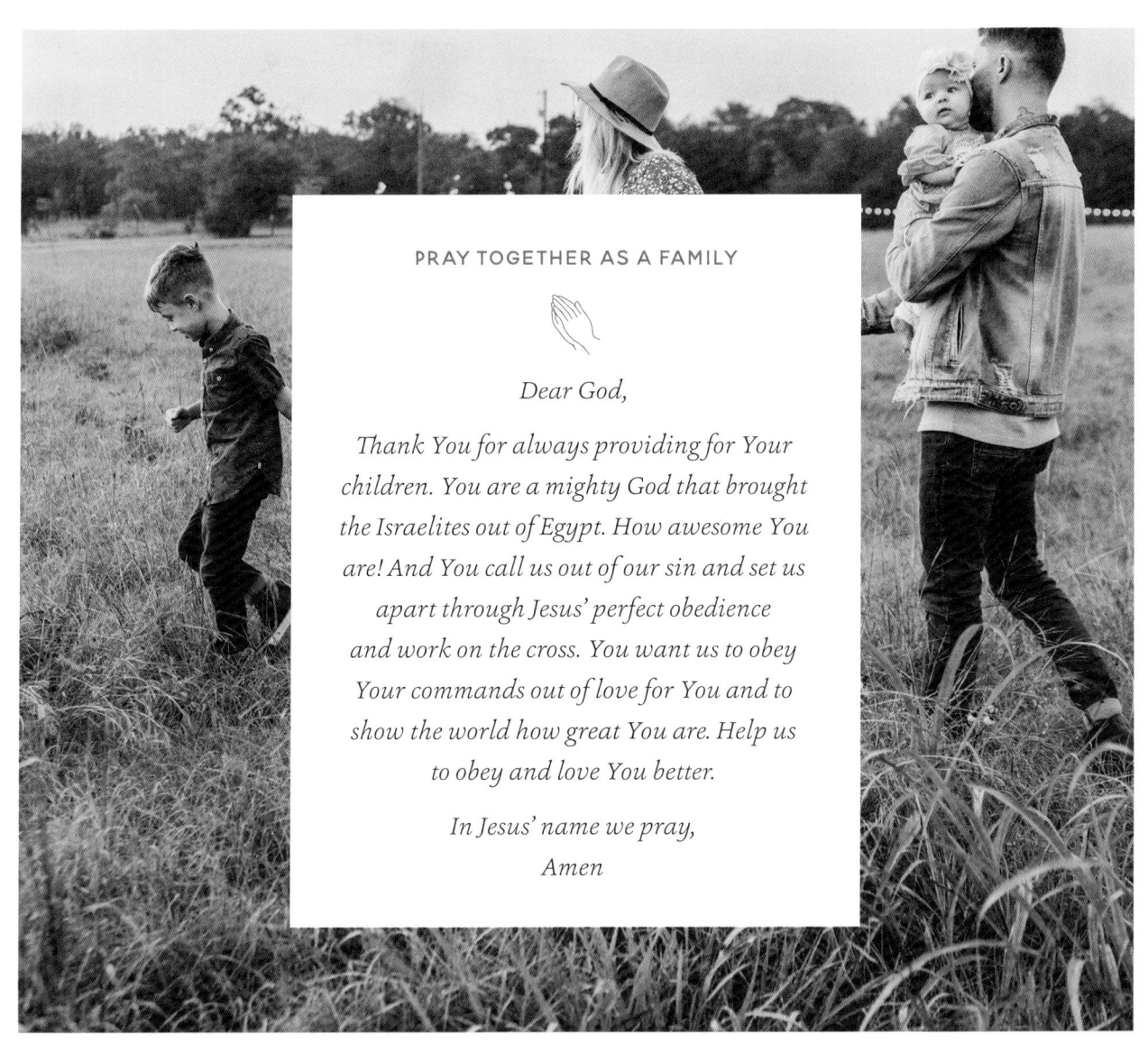

PRAY TOGETHER AS A FAMILY

Dear God,

Thank You for always providing for Your children. You are a mighty God that brought the Israelites out of Egypt. How awesome You are! And You call us out of our sin and set us apart through Jesus' perfect obedience and work on the cross. You want us to obey Your commands out of love for You and to show the world how great You are. Help us to obey and love You better.

In Jesus' name we pray,
Amen

1. When things got tough, the Israelites quickly forgot that God delivered them out of Egypt and began to grumble. When things get tough in your life, how do you tend to forget the good that God does and only complain about the bad?

2. God gave the ten commandments to show the Israelites (and us) how life works best. Jesus said in Matthew 22:40 that all of the Old Testament (the law and prophets) can be met by loving God and loving others. How are the ten commandments split up to help you love God and love others?

3. God knew that people couldn't perfectly obey His commandments. They show us our need for Jesus—the only sinless man that perfectly obeyed. But why are we still called to obey God?

LIVING AS
a Temple
OF GOD

At Mt. Sinai, God also told the Israelites to build a tabernacle, which was like a giant tent that would be a transportable sanctuary. This was a place where God would meet and dwell with His people. God gave very specific instructions of how this should be built; they just had to obey. Does this remind you of Noah and the ark? Well, there was another type of ark within the tabernacle called the ark of the covenant, and it was the most important piece of furniture in the tent. This is where the Israelites kept a copy of the ten commandments, and it was in the Most Holy Place. This was the holiest area because it was where God's presence resided. There would be purple curtains to symbolize royalty woven with blue scarlet yarn to symbolize divinity. God was very intentional of the placement of everything within the tent. In fact, if you really paid close attention, you would notice that things were set up in a way to make the Israelites think back to the garden of Eden. This was just another way God pointed them back to His grand plan. He would send the Promised Savior to restore what was lost and would dwell with His people again! The golden lampstand in the Holy Place remained lit and provided light for the priests. It pointed to Jesus because He is the true light that would come into the world (John 1:9) for all of us. God's plan was moving forward, and He was now present and near.

God appointed priests and gave them very specific duties. The priests would represent the people before God. And the animal sacrifices were a powerful symbol of God's justice and grace because the death of innocent animals were acceptable substitutes, symbolically dying for the sins of the people. This is called atonement. These sacrifices pointed to a greater sacrifice that was still to come in Jesus.

In the New Testament, God's people are called the Israel of God (Rom. 11:11-24). You see, Jesus's death offers us atonement for our sins, too. Because of Jesus, we can live in peace with God. He is the perfect sacrifice that all of the animal sacrifices pointed to. Jesus is the true and better tabernacle. The Apostle John wrote "the Word became flesh and dwelt among us" (John 1:14). He is saying that Jesus tabernacled among us. Jesus is our High Priest (Heb. 4:14), our Temple (John 2:21), and our King (Rev. 17:14). Because of Jesus, the old covenant is gone (Heb. 8:13). This means the priesthood, the sacrifices, and the tabernacle are no longer necessary because Jesus fulfilled it all. We have the New Covenant. As believers, we are the "chosen race, a royal priesthood, a holy nation, a people for His own possession" so that we can be an example of Him to the world (1 Peter 2:9). We have His Holy Spirit dwelling in us, making us a temple of God (1 Cor. 3:16).

BECAUSE OF JESUS, WE CAN LIVE IN PEACE WITH GOD. HE IS THE PERFECT SACRIFICE THAT ALL OF THE ANIMAL SACRIFICES POINTED TO. JESUS IS THE TRUE AND BETTER TABERNACLE.

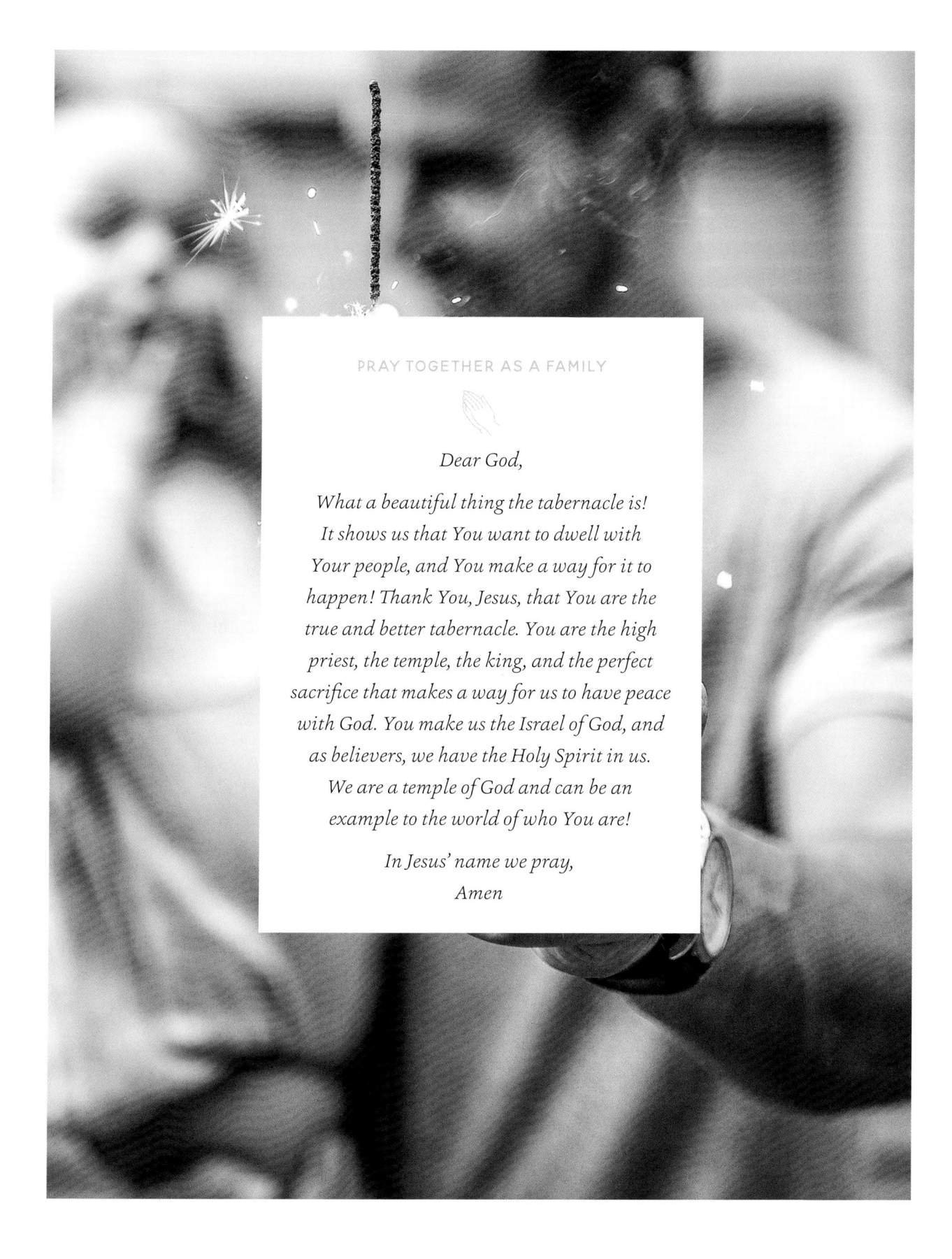

Dear God,

What a beautiful thing the tabernacle is! It shows us that You want to dwell with Your people, and You make a way for it to happen! Thank You, Jesus, that You are the true and better tabernacle. You are the high priest, the temple, the king, and the perfect sacrifice that makes a way for us to have peace with God. You make us the Israel of God, and as believers, we have the Holy Spirit in us. We are a temple of God and can be an example to the world of who You are!

In Jesus' name we pray,
Amen

1. What is so important about the ark of the covenant?

2. How does the tabernacle in the Old Testament make you think about Jesus, the true and better tabernacle?

3. If Jesus is your Lord and Savior, the Holy Spirit dwells in you, and you are a living temple of God. How does that change the way you think about your life right now?

Israel's
FAVORITE
SON

JUST GO!

KEEP THE Commandments

LIVING AS a Temple OF GOD

Make a Noise!

The Old Testament has a lot of laws, ceremonies, and rituals, and it may be hard to understand those things. They were actually guidelines that God gave His people so they would know how to worship and obey Him. God is holy and He was calling His covenant people to holiness too. So after receiving the Law and building the tabernacle, they continued toward the Promised Land with the ark of the covenant leading the way. The journey should have only taken two weeks on foot, but get this, it took 40 years! Yes, the Israelites spent 40 years in the wilderness because of unbelief. You see, God had led them to a place called Kadesh, and the Promised Land (which is called Canaan) was just across the Jordan River. Moses sent 12 spies to go check out the land. When they returned, ten of the spies caused an uproar. They told the Israelites that the people in Canaan were too strong and they wouldn't be able to overtake them. The other two spies, Caleb and Joshua, agreed that the people were big and strong, but they knew they would overcome them because God was on their side. After all, it was God's plan and promise to give them this very land.

But the Israelites grumbled against Moses. They even said they wished they would have died in Egypt or in the wilderness. They doubted God's goodness. Sounds like Adam and Eve in the garden, right? But Joshua encouraged the Israelites to not rebel against the Lord or fear the people because God would take away the Canaanites' protection and be with them instead (Num. 14:7-9). But they didn't listen. So God gave them what they wanted. God prevented them from going into the Promised Land by causing them to wander in the wilderness for 40 years until the unbelieving generation died (Joshua 5:6). From that generation, only Joshua and Caleb would go into the land. In that time, Moses died and Joshua was the new leader. It was time to get the Promised Land. Just as God started the Exodus by allowing the Israelites to miraculously walk across the Red Sea on dry ground, He ended the Exodus by providing them dry ground to cross the Jordan River into the Promised Land.

Now the first battle was before them. Jericho was a city built on a steep hill with two big walls surrounding it, and it was hard for attackers to successfully strike. But God had a battle plan for them. It would require complete trust from the Israelites because, truthfully, it didn't make any sense. For six days, everyone was going to march around the city walls once in complete silence. Seven priests, each blowing a ram's horn, would go in front of the ark. On the seventh day, they would march around seven times and when signaled, they would all make a loud noise –a big, unified shout that would cause the walls to come crashing down. Then they would go into the city, take all of the silver, gold, bronze, and iron and then burn the city down. Only one family would be saved: a lady named Rahab and her family. Rahab was a Canaanite, but she believed in the God of the Israelites.

This was the plan, and it worked. The Israelites overcame the Canaanites. This story is a picture of judgment. The city was completely destroyed because of their wickedness and unbelief. It is also a symbol of God's victory. But soon, our world will be judged and wickedness and evil will be destroyed. The Apostle Paul writes:

For the Lord himself will descend from heaven with a shout,
with the archangel's voice, and with the trumpet of God,
and the dead in Christ will rise first.
I THESSALONIANS 4:16

Just as Joshua ushered in the judgment to the Canaanites, one day, Jesus will bring judgment to the world. God will be victorious. Just as the priests' horns sounded and the people shouted, God's trumpet will sound one day and He will give a cry of command. Rahab and her family were saved because she turned from the ways of the Canaanites and put her faith in the God of the Hebrews. We can be saved when we put our faith in Jesus.

GOD IS HOLY AND HE WAS CALLING HIS
COVENANT PEOPLE TO HOLINESS TOO.

PRAY TOGETHER AS A FAMILY

Dear God,

You are gracious. When the Israelites grumbled yet again, You gave them what they wanted, even if that meant wandering in the wilderness for 40 years! Help us not grumble and miss out on the blessings You have planned for Your people! May we trust You, even if we don't understand the plan. May we be like Joshua and Caleb and obey, believing in your promises and protection. May we put our faith in Jesus and be ready for when the trumpet of God sounds!

In Jesus' name we pray,
Amen

1. Because the Israelites didn't believe God and His plan, the journey that should have only taken two weeks took 40 years! How does that make you think about God, His plan, and your obedience to Him?

2. This was a strange battle plan, but God wanted His people to trust Him. Has there ever been a time you had to trust God even if it didn't make sense in your own mind?

3. Jericho reminds us that all wickedness and evil will be judged and there will be a day when Jesus returns as a righteous judge. How can you get ready for the trumpet of God to sound?

Naomi, Ruth, and the KINSMAN REDEEMER

Joshua led the Israelites and conquered many areas of the Promised Land, but there were still many Canaanites left by the time of his death. There was a new generation of Israelites and their parents didn't teach them to "know the Lord or the work that he had done for Israel" (Judges 2:10). So instead of pursuing holiness to reflect their God, they were influenced by the culture and religion of the Canaanites. And during this time, they were governed by judges, who were more like military generals on a battlefield rather than lawyers in a courtroom. The judges were far from perfect, but God still used them to deliver His people time and time again. But Israel wanted a human king, and today's story will be about the beginnings of one of their future kings.

This story is about a lady named Ruth. She was a Moabite; she wasn't from one of the tribes of Israel. She married into an Israelite family, but sadly, her husband and the other men in the family died. Ruth could have left her mother-in-law, Naomi, to find a new husband. In fact, Naomi begged Ruth three times to go find a better life for herself. But Ruth refused and moved with Naomi to her family's hometown of Bethlehem.

Ruth told Naomi:

"Don't plead with me to abandon you or to return and not follow you. For wherever you go, I will go, and wherever you live, I will live; your people will be my people, and your God will be my God. Where you die, I will die, and there I will be buried. May the Lord punish me, and do so severely, if anything but death separates you and me."

RUTH 1:16-17

Ruth was loyal and she believed in the God of the Israelites and not the pagan god of the Moabites. She was a hard worker. She was willing to pick grain in the fields to provide food for them. You see, back then, Israelites were told to leave some grain in their fields for the poor to have. It just so happened that Ruth took grain from the field of Boaz. He was a wealthy, generous, and godly man. He saw Ruth's loyalty to Naomi, and he was impressed and gave her favor. Ruth didn't know it, but Boaz was also a close family relative and could be their kinsman redeemer. Now what is a kinsman redeemer? This was a part of Israel's law that said an unmarried man in an Israelite family should marry a widow within that family in order to take care of the family. This man would "redeem" this family by marrying her and giving her a son in order to carry on the family name. Boaz was unmarried, and he was godly and upheld the law. He was willing to be the redeemer, but he realized that there was a closer relative that would have the right to the special marriage before him. As it turned out, that person was unwilling so Boaz stepped up. And this is what is incredible: Boaz and Ruth had a son named Obed, and he is the grandfather of Israel's future king named David. Does King David sound familiar? Yep, it is from this King David's family line that Jesus, the Promised Savior, would come!

Boaz is a type (picture) of Christ. Boaz was the kinsman redeemer and had the ability and willingness to save these widows. Jesus is our redeemer, and He was the only one with the ability to save us and He willingly did. Ruth was a Moabite. She came from a country that was very hostile toward the Israelites. It was a country that was even cursed by God. This meant Ruth, as a Moabite, was a foreigner and enemy of Israel. Yet she believed in the

God of Israel. She was redeemed and even included in the genealogy of the Messiah, Jesus. We, too, can believe in God and be redeemed through Jesus. Jesus willingly became a curse for us by taking our sins and made a way for us to go from enemy of God to child of God.

THIS IS A BEAUTIFUL STORY OF GOD'S REDEEMING GRACE FOR ALL OF US AND A REMINDER THAT HE USES HUMAN DECISIONS AND ACTIONS TO FULFILL HIS REDEMPTIVE PURPOSES.

PRAY TOGETHER AS A FAMILY

Dear God,

Thank You for this beautiful story that reminds us that You are in control and kind. You didn't forget about Naomi or Ruth. You provided a kinsman redeemer for them and even let them be in Your grand plan in the family tree of Jesus, the Promised Savior. Thank You that Jesus is our Redeemer. Thank You, Jesus, for becoming a curse for us and making a way for us to be in the family of God, too.

In Jesus' name we pray,
Amen

1. Your parents want to teach you to know the Lord. Reading the Bible helps you know God because the passages teach you about His character, like His faithfulness in this story. How does reading the Bible help you resist the influence of the culture around you?

2. After Naomi and Ruth became widows, Naomi was bitter. She felt like God's hand was against her. But then Boaz showed up, and then she saw that God was kind and always provided. How have you seen God provide in a situation that seemed hopeless?

3. Ruth was a foreigner, and being a Moabite, she was an enemy of the Israelites and cursed. But she believed in God, and she ended up being in the genealogy of Jesus. What does that tell you about God and His plan of redemption?

ONE SMALL STONE

For a time, Israel was ruled by judges. Israel's last judge was Samuel, and we'll start today's story with him. Samuel was also a prophet, and when Israel demanded a king "like all the nations" (1 Sam. 8:5), he talked to God. God told Samuel to anoint a king because Israel had rejected God as king over them. Now, God knew that this would happen! So a man named Saul was appointed the first king of Israel, and he was tall and handsome and looked like the perfect king. But he wasn't. He was full of pride and didn't always do what was right and honest. He seemed like a good king at first, but then he disobeyed God, and God told Samuel that Israel needed a new king. He told Samuel to go to Bethlehem and find the next king in Jesse's family.

Now Jesse was Ruth's grandson, and he had eight sons. Samuel thought it would be Jesse's firstborn because he looked like a king. He was tall, strong, and handsome. But God told Samuel that a good leader was more of a matter of the heart. Do you know who God chose? God chose the youngest and the smallest of the brothers, David, a shepherd boy. Samuel anointed David right away, and the Bible says, "the Spirit of the Lord came powerfully upon David from that day forward" (1 Sam. 16:13) and the Spirit would empower him. This was God's brilliant way of bringing David into Saul's royal staff. You see, whenever David played his musical instrument, the evil spirit stopped bothering Saul, which made Saul love David. David was then made an armor-bearer while still shepherding his dad's sheep. One day, David's dad told him to take his older brothers, who were soldiers in Saul's army, some lunch. When David got to the valley, he noticed something: all of the Israelite soldiers were very afraid. You see, the Philistines were enemies of Israel and they had a secret weapon—a giant named Goliath. He was over nine feet tall and he was super strong. His armor coat was over 100lbs! For 40 days, this giant walked out every morning and every evening and challenged the Israelites to a battle. But not just any battle—a one-on-one fight! The loser's team would have to become the other team's slaves. Not one soldier in Saul's army was brave enough to face him. But David saw what was really going on. Goliath was challenging Israel's God, and David knew he had God's help. So guess what he did? He volunteered to fight Goliath. Saul gave David fancy battle gear, but it was too heavy for David. Instead, David got his staff, sling, and five stones tucked into his shepherd's pouch. David boldly walked up to the battle field, and this is what he said to Goliath:

Today, the Lord will hand you over to me. Today, I'll strike you down, remove your head, and give the corpses of the Philistine camp to the birds of the sky and the wild creatures of the earth. Then all the world will know that Israel has a God, and this whole assembly will know that it is not by sword or by spear that the Lord saves, for the battle is the Lord's. He will hand you over to us.
I SAMUEL 17:46-47

With one stone, David defeated Goliath and the Philistines all ran away in terror! Again, the power of the one, true God was clear. And again, we see a type of Jesus in David. David was a shepherd. He willingly risked his life to battle bears and lions that threatened his dad's lambs. And after he was appointed by Samuel to be Israel's future king, he risked his life to battle Goliath in order to shepherd the people of Israel against the threat of the Philistines. He fought alone and brought victory for his people. Jesus is the true and better David. He is our ultimate Shepherd and won our battle against our enemy, sin (1 Cor. 15:57). And He freely gives His victory to us.

PRAY TOGETHER AS A FAMILY

Dear God,

Thank You for not looking at people's outward appearances but looking at our hearts. Help us to be pure of heart — humble and patient, like David. Whatever battles we face in our lives, may we boldly stand on Your truth. Thank You, Jesus, for fighting the ultimate battle for us, and thank You for sharing your victory with us. Thank You for being our Shepherd.

In Jesus' name we pray,
Amen

1. Saul was the first king of Israel, and he looked like a king. But God was teaching His people that His warriors are strong and mighty because of what is inside their hearts. Do you tend to focus on your outward appearance more than your heart?

2. What made David so brave against the Philistines and Goliath?

3. Jesus fought our battle against sin and won on the cross, and He gives us His victory. How does knowing that Jesus already won the battle for you help you fight the everyday battle against sin in your heart?

PREACH
the Good News
TO YOUR ENEMIES!

David was a man after God's own heart (1 Sam. 13:14), and he was a great king. Under David's leadership, Israel's tribes were united as one kingdom. He conquered Jerusalem and made it a great capital for the Israelites. David wanted to make a temple for God's presence, but God told David that He didn't want him to make a house for God. Instead, God told David the grand plan—God was going to make a house of David and a royal lineage (2 Sam. 7:12). Through the Davidic covenant, David was told that the Messiah would come through his family: "And your house and your kingdom shall be made sure forever before me. Your throne shall be established forever." (1 Sam. 7:16). Remember what the angel said that very first Christmas? "The Lord God will give him the throne of his father David, and he will reign over the house of Jacob forever, and of his kingdom there will be no end" (Luke 1:32–33). This forever would be fulfilled in Jesus!

But in the meantime, David's son, Solomon, took over as king. As you may have heard, Solomon asked God for wisdom, which made God happy. Solomon became very rich, too, and built God a temple. But Solomon disobeyed God, and the kingdom split into twelve tribes. The northern kingdom (Israel) was made up of ten tribes and the southern kingdom (Judah) was made up of two tribes. Today's story comes from the northern kingdom with a prophet named Jonah. You may have about the prophet that was swallowed by a whale. What's that about? Let's start from the beginning. Jonah was a prophet, which meant he received special words from God for the people. But this is more about what Jonah didn't say. You see, God told Jonah to go to a big city called Nineveh, and it happened to be the capital of Israel's big enemy. Jonah disobeyed and hopped on a boat going the opposite direction. But, of course, God's plan doesn't depend on our obedience. God hurled a powerful storm at them, so powerful that it scared the professional sailors on the boat. They did something interesting. They cast lots to figure out who was to blame for this misfortune. Jonah ended up telling them to throw him into the sea to save themselves because he really didn't want to go to Nineveh! But he didn't die. Instead, God made a great fish swallow him, and Jonah spent three days and nights in the fish's belly. There, Jonah prayed and told God he would go to Nineveh. Interestingly, once Jonah got to Nineveh, he preached the world's shortest sermon. It is only 5 words in Hebrew! He said,

> *"In forty days Nineveh will be demolished!"*
> JONAH 3:4B

He didn't even preach it around the whole city, but do you know what happened? Everyone repented! Now, Jonah got angry and his second prayer was full of complaints. He groaned, "I knew that you are a gracious and compassionate God, slow to anger, abounding in faithful love, and one who relents from sending disaster." He pouted and went out of the city. Do you know why he got so angry? He didn't like that God would forgive these people. These are people that were not from Israel, and even more, they were brutal enemies of Israel!

But here's how this story ends. God kindly used a plant to teach Jonah a lesson. He showed Jonah how selfish he was. And in turn, God showed His

deep love, mercy, and concern for all people, and this is good news for us. It's easy to see how Jesus is the true and better Jonah. More than Jonah's three days and nights in the belly of a fish, Jesus spent three days and nights in the "heart of the earth" (Matt. 12:40). Jonah being spit out from the belly of the fish enable a nation to repent and draw near to the Lord. When Jesus burst forth from the grave, He declared victory over the grave and eternal life for all who would believe. Jesus wasn't concerned with his own comfort; He willingly left his heavenly home to calm the ultimate storm in our lives caused by the waves of sin. He threw himself into our storm and laid down his life for us while we were His enemies!

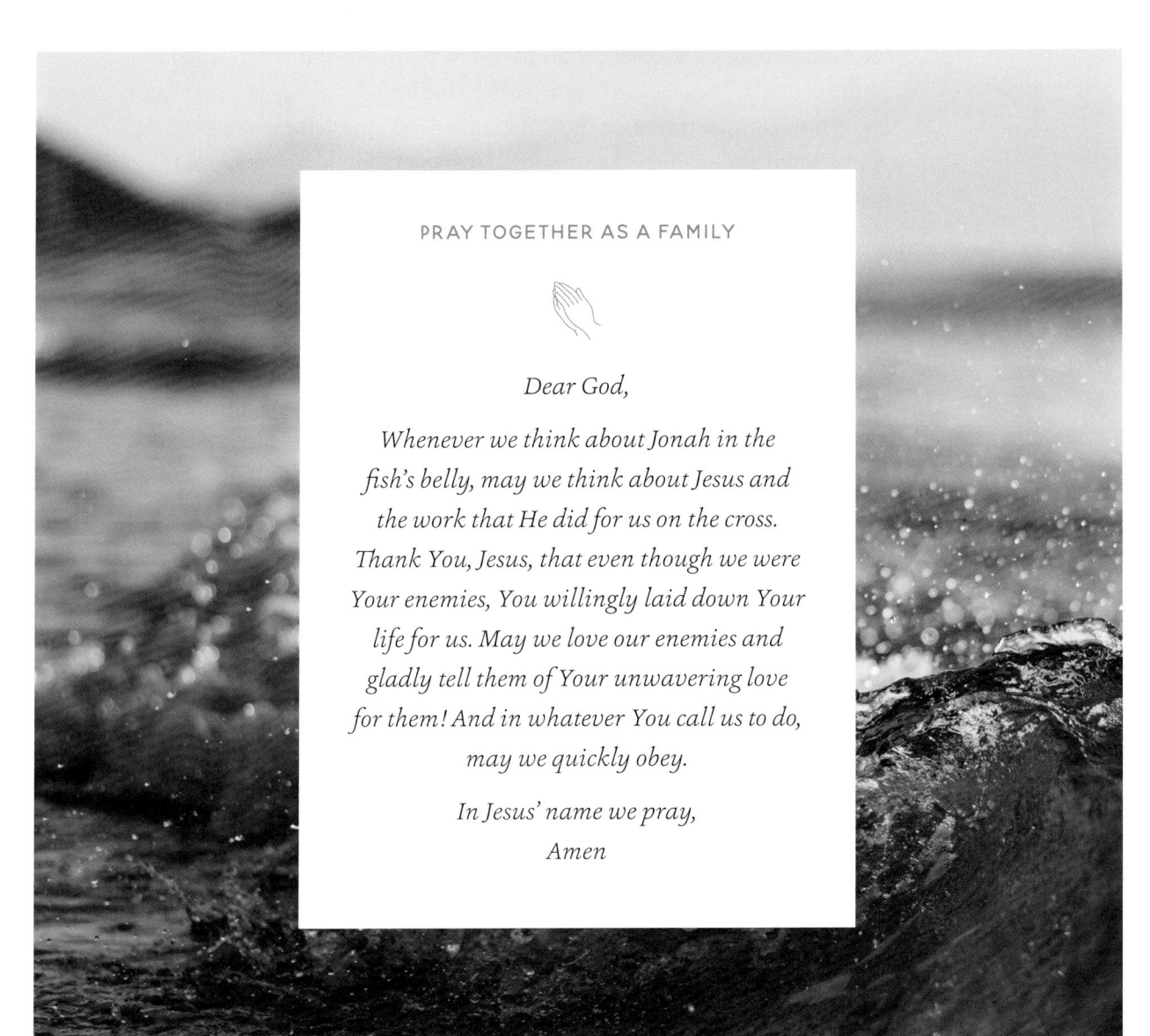

PRAY TOGETHER AS A FAMILY

Dear God,

Whenever we think about Jonah in the fish's belly, may we think about Jesus and the work that He did for us on the cross. Thank You, Jesus, that even though we were Your enemies, You willingly laid down Your life for us. May we love our enemies and gladly tell them of Your unwavering love for them! And in whatever You call us to do, may we quickly obey.

In Jesus' name we pray,
Amen

1. Jonah didn't want to preach the good news to Israel's enemies. In fact, he got angry that God gave His love and mercy to the Ninevites. Are there people that you sometimes think are unworthy of God's love and mercy?

2. This story reminds us that God's deep love, mercy, and concern are for all people. How can you show the love of Christ to someone that is completely different from you?

3. Jesus is the true and better Jonah. He laid down His life for us, His enemies. How can you better love your enemy?

Make a Noise!

Naomi, Ruth, and THE KINSMAN REDEEMER

ONE SMALL STORY

PREACH
the Good News
TO YOUR ENEMIES!

a QUESTIONABLE Bride

So the Ninevites repented, which allowed Israel to have some relief from their great enemy, the Assyrians. Instead of growing in their faith, they turned away from God! They wondered, "Why do we need God if we are now friends with mighty nations like Egypt and Assyria?"

So this is where today's story begins. It was about 200 years after the division of God's special nation into two kingdoms. And today's prophet, Hosea, was in the northern kingdom. God was going to share a message to His people through Hosea's life. God saw that all of the kings in the northern kingdom were unfaithful, corrupt, and supported the worship of idols. So God used prophets to remind the people of God's commands and His special calling on Israel to be holy. But God wasn't going to just give Hosea words to say to His people. No, God was going to use Hosea's personal life to show Israel the depth of His love.

This story is a living, prophetic symbol. You see, God told Hosea to do something strange. Hosea was told to marry a specific woman who was impure and had a bad reputation for being unfaithful (she would be an adulteress). God wanted the prophet to marry her and start a family with her. So God wanted Hosea to have a covenant relationship with an unfaithful bride. Do you see what's going on? God is in a covenant relationship with Israel, but they were unfaithful — like Gomer was to Hosea. But just as God called Hosea to love her unconditionally, so God also loves His people with a covenant love that will never be broken. But in the process, Hosea was going to experience a little taste of the pain that God was enduring with Israel's unfaithfulness. So Hosea obeyed. He married a woman named Gomer, and they had three children. His kids were given names with interesting meanings: "God Will Scatter," "No Mercy," and "Not My People." Basically, God was saying that Israel was no longer His people and He was not their God (Hosea 1:9) because they were worshiping foreign gods and breaking the ten commandments. But, as you'll see, God isn't like man; He doesn't respond to unfaithfulness with abandonment.

So as God said, Gomer was unfaithful and she was "loved by another man" (Hosea 3:1). But God told Hosea to go again and love her. Hosea was to respond to his wife's unfaithfulness with a renewed love. He was told to go, even though she left him for someone else. He was supposed to go win her back. And he did! But Hosea also wrote truth to the Israelites in the form of poetry. He told them of God's judgment that was going to come. You see, there are consequences to sin. And it came! Israel was conquered by the Assyrians as God used Assyria as a rod of His anger (Isa. 10:5).

BUT HOSEA'S POETRY ALSO REMINDED THEM OF TRUE HOPE BECAUSE GOD IS COMMITTED TO HIS COVENANT LOVE:

How can I give you up, Ephraim? How can I surrender you, Israel? How can I make you like Admah? How can I treat you like Zeboiim? I have had a change of heart; my compassion is stirred! I will not vent the full fury of my anger; I will not turn back to destroy Ephraim. For I am God and not man, the Holy One among you; I will not come in rage.
HOSEA 11:8-9

You see, Hosea called for Israel to repent, but he knew they would fail again. So he told them that God was going to heal them and save them, but this wouldn't fully be seen until Jesus comes back and brings the New Jerusalem that will be better than Eden. You see, God is showing us that the salvation of His people is more than just freedom from the curse of sin and death. He is devoted to us, and the best way to live is to obey Him. We won't be able to obey perfectly, but Jesus obeyed perfectly in our place. And He's coming back again, and we will be with Him forever.

PRAY TOGETHER AS A FAMILY

Dear God,

Thank You for this story of Hosea and Gomer that is a living symbol of Your covenant love for us. Even though there are consequences to sin, You remind us that You will never abandon us because of our unfaithfulness. We can rest in Your covenant love and mercy! But help us to live a faithful life and obey Your commands. Thank You that Jesus will come again and we will be fully healed and united with You in glory.

In Jesus' name we pray,
Amen

1. God chose to use Hosea's personal life as a living symbol of His love for His people. How does Hosea and Gomer's marriage represent God's covenant love and commitment to His people?

2. Hosea told Israel to repent, but he knew they would mess up. Even still, the very last verse in the book of Hosea reminds us that there are two ways of living – in obedience or disobedience. Obeying God is the wise way. How can we live wisely today?

3. This story reminds us that we won't ever perfectly obey until Jesus comes back. This is what our current season of waiting is all about. We are waiting for Jesus to come back again. How can we prepare our hearts for Jesus' second coming?

RESTORATION & God's remnant

Now there was another important prophet back in those days named Isaiah, and his message was mainly for the southern kingdom of Judah. The capital of Judah was Jerusalem, and its kings came from the line of King David. Unfortunately, this kingdom was also marked by spiritual corruption. They had a couple of kings that worshiped the one true God and tried to live as God's covenant people, but overall, Judah struggled to stay spiritually pure. So Isaiah was given a message from God for His people, and the big idea of his message was summed up in the meaning of Isaiah's name: "The Lord saves".

You see, Isaiah warned Israel that judgment was coming. Assyria and then Babylon would overtake them. This is because sin has consequences. Judah's idolatry, rebellion, and pride would not go unpunished. But Isaiah's message was beautiful because while he told them of the coming judgment, he also told them about God's grace for those that repent and put their faith in Him. More than any of the other prophets, Isaiah's message of salvation is rooted in the sending of a Messiah. Isaiah pointed directly to Jesus as the Promised Savior. And even more, Isaiah talked about the New Jerusalem that Jesus would establish after His second coming, which is what we're waiting for right now.

God always speaks good news into bad news (like He did with Adam and Even in Gen. 3:15). So even though Jerusalem would be destroyed, God promised them a remnant (a small group of people) that would be saved because of God's covenant faithfulness (Isa. 6:13).

But can you believe no one listened to him? Even though many of Isaiah's prophecies came true in his own lifetime, God knew that the people's hearts would be hardened and they wouldn't see the truth. But Isaiah obeyed and continued to preach. He preached that judgment is coming but also reminded the people that there is hope. After Isaiah died, his other prophecies came true. One hundred years later, the defeat and exile of Judah happened by Babylon under the leadership of King Nebuchadnezzar. But Isaiah also wrote about a man named Cyrus that would be used to gather the remnant of Israel back to the land (Isa. 44:28). Fast forward another 50 years, and King Cyrus of Persia overthrew Babylon and then was prompted by God to allow the Israelites in exile to return to Jerusalem!

So why does all of that matter to us today? You see, a large chunk of Isaiah's writing focuses on the Servant and the messianic kingdom that He will establish. This servant is Jesus. It is through Jesus that all of the covenants would be fulfilled. Through Him, Israel will be restored (Isa. 49:5). Jesus is "the light for the nations" (Isa. 49:6). Isaiah even wrote how this will come about. Jesus would be despised, rejected, and crucified to His death in our place:

But he was pierced because of our rebellion, crushed because of our iniquities; punishment for our peace was on him, and we are healed by his wounds.

ISAIAH 53:5

This verse was fulfilled by Jesus at the cross. But He rose again! Isaiah also wrote a lot about Jesus' second coming. Israel's future kingdom will come and Jesus will sit on David's throne on earth as king (Isa. 55:3). This is what our Advent is all about—waiting for Jesus to come back. When we celebrate Christmas each year, we affirm the fulfillment that Isaiah talked about regarding Jesus' first Advent. The Messiah was born of a virgin and called Immanuel, meaning "God with us" (Isa. 7:14). He was God in human flesh and born to bring peace on earth (Isa. 9:6). At Easter we celebrate that Jesus suffered and died for the sins of His people. And now, we expectantly wait for the fulfillment of Isaiah's words regarding Jesus' second coming. He will come back!

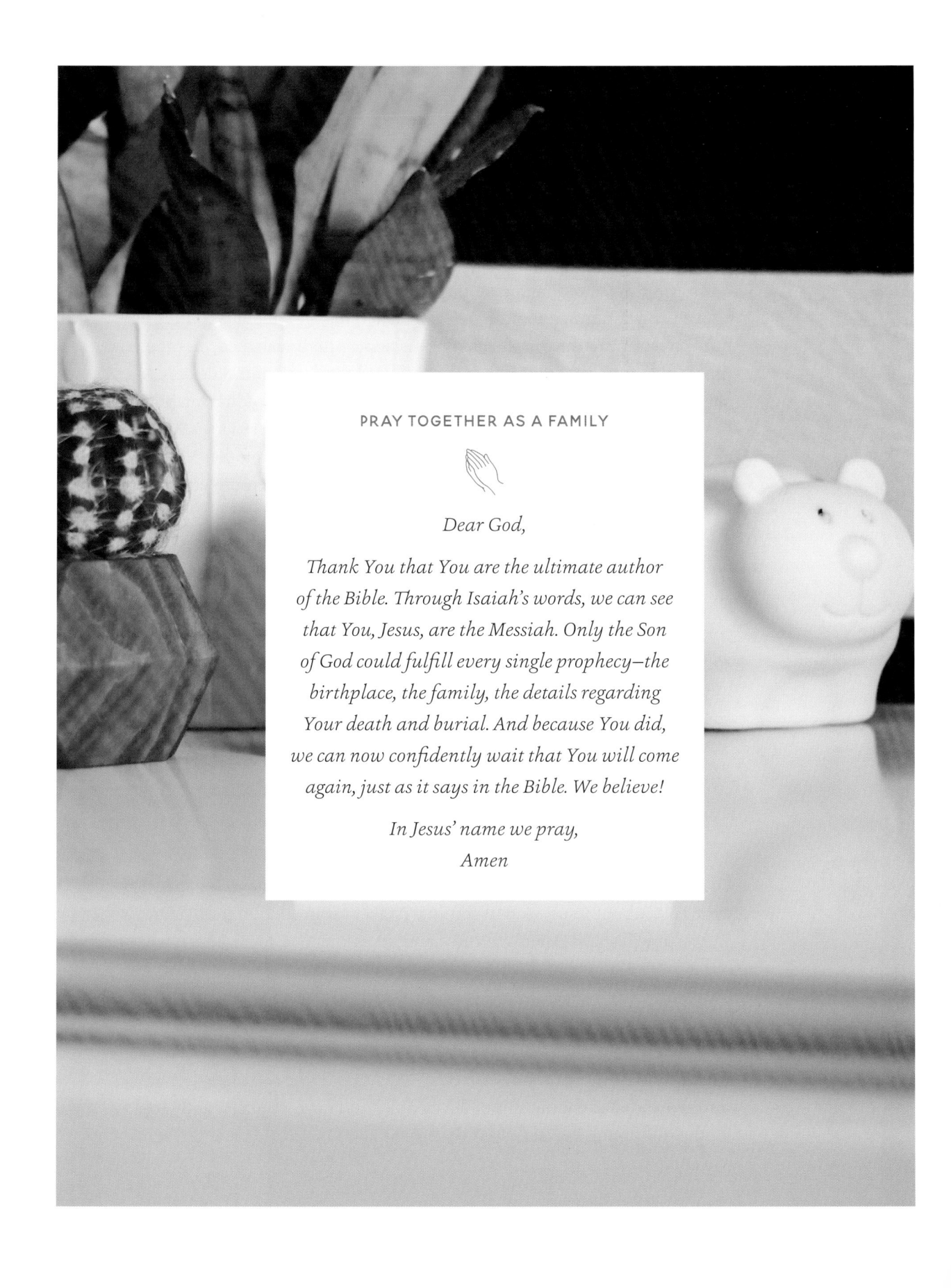

PRAY TOGETHER AS A FAMILY

Dear God,

Thank You that You are the ultimate author of the Bible. Through Isaiah's words, we can see that You, Jesus, are the Messiah. Only the Son of God could fulfill every single prophecy—the birthplace, the family, the details regarding Your death and burial. And because You did, we can now confidently wait that You will come again, just as it says in the Bible. We believe!

In Jesus' name we pray,
Amen

1. Isaiah's message was about judgment and hope. Why was Isaiah's message on hope so beautiful?

2. Israel's exile to Babylon was a result of judgment because of their sin, but God had a plan to restore them. God built up Persia to overcome the Babylonians, and He told the King of Persia to let the Israelites return to Jerusalem. What does this tell you about God's character?

3. Because Isaiah's prophecies about Jesus' first coming were true, we can expectantly wait for Jesus' second coming. When He returns, He will establish His kingdom on earth. Are you ready for Jesus to come back?

SHADRACH, MESHACH, AND ABEDNEGO

Isaiah told Judah's kings that Babylon would defeat them as a judgment for their spiritual impurity, and 100 years later, it happened! Today's story begins after Babylon's first attack on Jerusalem, the capital of Judah. The Israelites were taken into exile in waves, and Daniel and his friends were in the first group. His friends were named Shadrach, Meshach, and Abednego. They were young Israelites from high class families. They were physically attractive, mentally sharp, and socially acceptable (Dan. 1:3-4). This was important because they were going to be intensely trained for three years for royal positions in Babylon. A key part of the training was for the young Israelites to abandon their religious loyalty to the God of Israel and to identify with the local gods. But these four friends refused to compromise their beliefs. Part of the training required them to eat and drink certain things that the king ate. Now, you might think this was a special privilege because they got to eat what the king ate. But the food and drink were devoted to the Babylonian gods, which were idols. If they ate and drank of them, they would be honoring the false gods. Plus, they were probably foods that were prohibited in the Israelite Law. Daniel was committed to the God of Israel, and he boldly asked if he and his friends could eat something else to prevent defilement. The Bible says God gave Daniel favor and compassion with his supervisors, and they allowed Daniel and his friends to eat vegetables instead. And throughout the training, God gave these faithful teens wisdom and understanding that surpassed the other trainees.

One day, King Nebuchadnezzar had a crazy dream. God helped Daniel interpret it for him when no one else could. But in response to the interpretation, the king ordered a giant, 90-foot image of gold to show off his own greatness. And not only that, but the Babylonian leaders also commanded everyone in the land to "fall down and worship" the image whenever they heard music (Dan. 3:4). If someone didn't, the consequence would be death in a burning fiery furnace. It wasn't long before some jealous priests used this as a trap to get rid of Shadrach, Meshach, and Abednego, who were appointed over the affairs of Babylon. They conveniently saw them refusing to fall down and worship the image at the sound of the music, and they told the king. The king was angry and challenged the three Israelites: if you don't worship it, you will immediately be thrown into a furnace of blazing fire – and who is the god who can rescue you from my power?" (Dan. 3:15). This was their reply:

If the God we serve exists, then he can rescue us from the furnace of blazing fire, and he can rescue us from the power of you, the king. But even if he does not rescue us, we want you as king to know that we will not serve your gods or worship the gold statue you set up.

DANIEL 3:17-18

The king's mighty men bound them up, and they took them to the furnace. The flames were so hot, the king's men were killed, and the three bound Israelites fell into the furnace. But then the king saw something in the fire. He didn't just see the three men, but now he saw four! They were unbound and untouched by the fire. The king told them to come out, and when they did, not a single hair on their head was singed. They didn't even smell of fire! Don't your clothes smell of fire even when you just sit next to a small fire pit? This was a miracle only God could do! The three were promoted and the king recognized the God of Israel. But how does this story point our hearts to Jesus? You see, Shadrach, Meshach, and Abednego were in an impossible and hopeless situation, but they trusted that God would deliver them. And He did. He sent a Rescuer to protect them from the flames. When it comes to our sins, we are in an impossible and hopeless situation, too. And the consequence of sin is death and, without the Rescuer, this means forever in a place with powerful flames, too. But God did send a Rescuer to save us from the impossible. This Rescuer is Jesus! We can look to Him to deliver us, and He has the power to unbind the chains of sin so we can live for Him.

Dear God,

Thank You for sending the perfect Rescuer to save us from the impossible and hopeless reality of our sins. We are unable to pay the penalty for our sins. You knew that, and so it was Your grand plan from the very beginning to send Jesus to pay the price. Thank you, Jesus, for offering Your victory to us! Like Daniel and his friends, may we remain faithful in a world that pressures us to compromise our faith. May we commit to serving You, the only living God, and refuse to bow down to any idols.

In Jesus' name we pray,
Amen

1. Daniel and his friends did not compromise their faith to fit into the world. Can you think of a time when you were tempted to do something just because everyone else was doing it, even though you knew God wouldn't be happy about it?

_____

_____

_____

_____

_____

2. Shadrach, Meshach, and Abednego were in a hopeless situation when they faced the burning fiery furnace, but they trusted God and He rescued them. How is Jesus the Rescuer in our impossible situation against sin?

_____

_____

_____

_____

_____

_____

3. Before being thrown into the fire, the three friends told the king that they would still only worship the one true God even if the flames burned them up. Our faith in God should not be swayed by our circumstances. How does that challenge you?

_____

_____

_____

_____

_____

_____

Tamed Lions

Like his friends, Daniel remained faithful to the God of Israel. And also like his friends, Daniel was in an impossible situation in need of God's rescue. That is today's story. After interpreting King Nebuchadnezzar's first dream, Daniel was appointed to be "ruler over the entire province of Babylon and chief governor over all the wise men of Babylon" (Dan. 2:48). It wasn't the last time that Daniel would use the gift God gave him—the gift of understanding visions and dreams. It was through dreams that God warned the kings of Babylon of the judgment that would come if they didn't repent of their pride. And it was Daniel that was the only one able to interpret the dreams for them. Unfortunately, neither kings humbled themselves immediately and judgment came, and the kingdom moved on to a man named Darius. Under Darius' rule, Daniel became a favorite because he had a spirit of excellence, and the people who worked with Daniel were jealous of him. They made plans to trap Daniel, and they knew the only way to make Daniel fall was to tempt him to do something against the law of his God (Dan. 6:5).

So they made a plan. They flattered King Darius and got him to sign a document that said no one was supposed to pray to any god or man for thirty days. They could only pray to the king. If not, the consequence would be death by being cast into a lion's den! Daniel knew about this new rule and the consequence, but he didn't stop praying to the God of Israel. No matter what, Daniel prayed three times a day, and the scheming men knew this. So of course, it wasn't long before they caught Daniel praying to the God of Israel, and they told the king. Unfortunately, even though the king really, really liked Daniel and didn't want him thrown in the lion's den, he knew that he couldn't go back on the document he signed. So this is what he said to Daniel:

> *"May your God, whom you serve continually, deliver you!"*
> DANIEL 6:16B

Daniel was then thrown in the lion's den, and a rock sealed the opening. But the king had hope in Daniel's God. Early the next morning, he rushed to the lion's den and called out to Daniel. Do you know what happened? God protected Daniel from the lions. He didn't even have a scratch! Daniel told the king that God had sent an angel to shut the lions' mouths. Amazing! But then the king threw the scheming men and their families into the den because they tricked him with the silly document to get what they wanted. And guess what! The lions devoured them before they even reached the bottom of the den! This showed that Daniel's protection from the lions was a miracle only God could do! It wasn't that the lions weren't hungry or that they were naturally tame when it was Daniel's turn in the den. No, the living God of Israel tamed the lions for His own glory! So King Darius recognized the God of Israel and said:

> *For he is the living God, and he endures forever; his kingdom*
> *will never be destroyed, and his dominion has no end.*
> *He rescues and delivers!*
> DANIEL 6:26-27A

Daniel was in an impossible and hopeless situation, and he needed God to deliver him. He needed a Rescuer. He couldn't stop the lions from pouncing on him. He couldn't crawl out. He couldn't tame them on his own. And God

sent a Rescuer to save him. Just like Daniel, our sin puts us in a hopeless and impossible situation. Sin can devour us and kill us. And God did send a Rescuer to save us from our sin. This Rescuer is Jesus! And after Jesus resurrected, He sent the Holy Spirit to empower us to overcome the power of sin. With Him, we can rule over sin and live a life that brings Him glory!

DANIEL'S PROTECTION FROM THE LIONS WAS A MIRACLE ONLY GOD COULD DO!

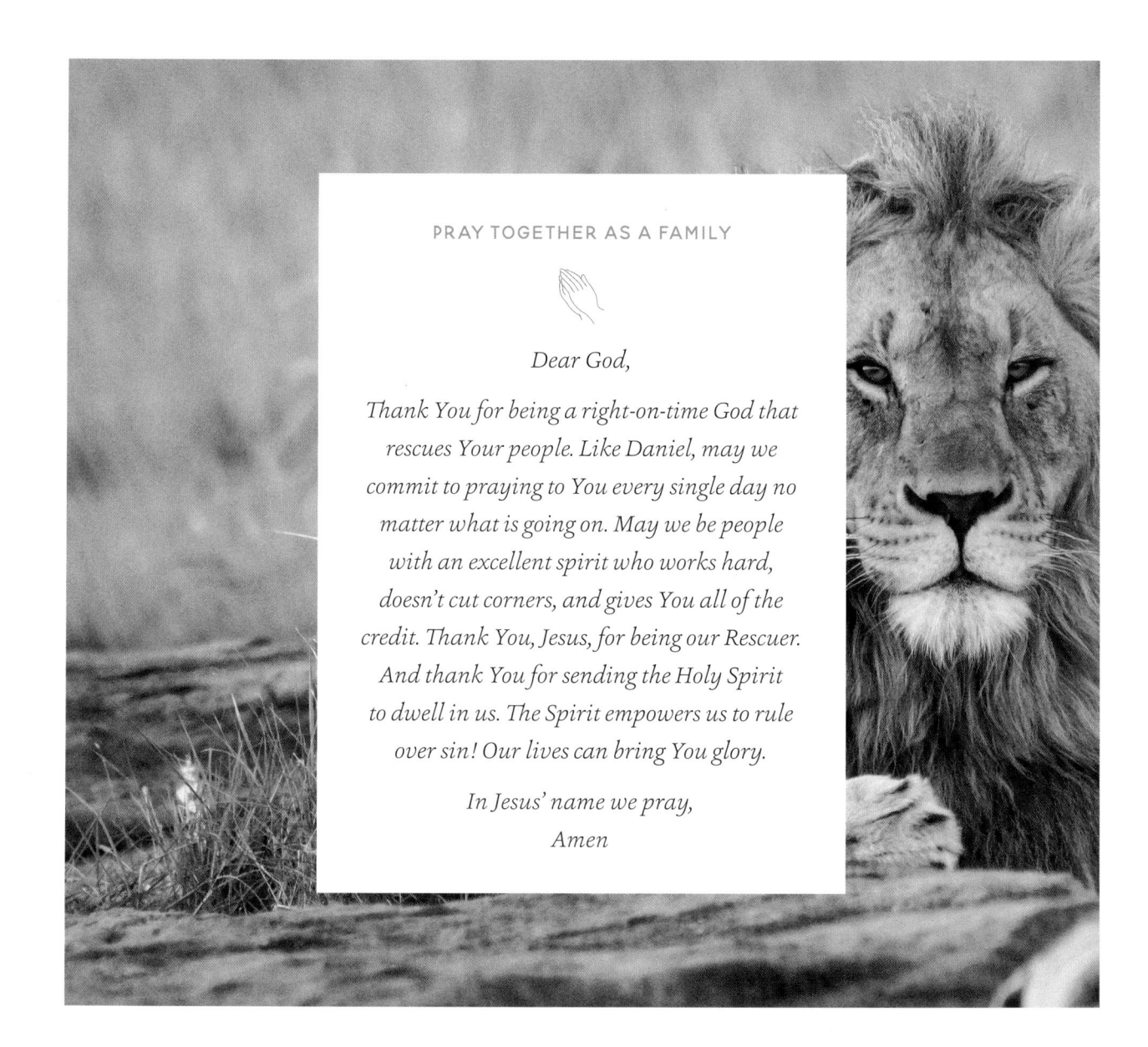

PRAY TOGETHER AS A FAMILY

Dear God,

Thank You for being a right-on-time God that rescues Your people. Like Daniel, may we commit to praying to You every single day no matter what is going on. May we be people with an excellent spirit who works hard, doesn't cut corners, and gives You all of the credit. Thank You, Jesus, for being our Rescuer. And thank You for sending the Holy Spirit to dwell in us. The Spirit empowers us to rule over sin! Our lives can bring You glory.

In Jesus' name we pray,
Amen

1. Daniel was an excellent worker and he always gave God the credit. We can do excellent work at school and home and give God glory, too. How does Daniel's example challenge you in your everyday life?

_____

_____

_____

_____

_____

2. Daniel prayed to God, just as he always did, even though he knew it may cost him his life. He refused to hide his faith. Share about a time when you felt the desire to hide your faith from the world.

_____

_____

_____

_____

_____

_____

3. This story reminds us that we have the third person in the Trinity—the Holy Spirit. While we wait for Jesus to come back, the Spirit helps us fight against sin. Have you ever asked the Holy Spirit to help you overcome temptations?

_____

_____

_____

_____

_____

_____

a QUESTIONABLE Bride

RESTORATION & God's remnant

SHADRACH, MESHACH, AND ABEDNEGO

Tamed Lions

UNDER GOD'S *Control*

In the story of Daniel, the Israelites were still in exile. Well, after 70 years, the captivity ended under King Cyrus of Persia, just as Isaiah had prophesied (Isa. 44:28). So in three waves, many of the Israelites returned to Jerusalem. Today's story falls in between the first two waves, and it's about a woman named Esther. She was living with her cousin, Mordecai, in one of the capitals of Persia. They were Israelites that were not returning to Jerusalem. In fact, they lived almost 1,000 miles away! But as we'll see, our God is big, and He protects His people wherever they are. And we'll see how God used Esther to save His covenant people even from afar.

The king of Persia at the time was named Ahasuerus, and he was looking for a new queen. Now, Esther was very beautiful, and a perfect candidate. Mordecai told her not to tell anyone that she was an Israelite because not everyone liked them. So Esther kept it a secret during her one-year training. Out of many women, Esther was chosen to be the queen. But there was a very important official that worked for the king named Haman. One day, Haman got into a squabble with Mordecai because Mordecai refused to bow down to him. Haman was angry, and when he realized that Mordecai was an Israelite, he made plans to "destroy all of Mordecai's people, the Jews, throughout Ahasuerus's kingdom" (Esther 3:6).

Haman schemed and convinced the king to approve a law to get rid of a certain people in the land. He told the king that they didn't follow the king's laws and it would be in the king's best interest to get rid of them. And guess what? The king agreed! Mordecai and the Jews across Persia mourned. And Mordecai told Esther to talk to the king to defend the Israelites. But even though Esther was the queen, if she approached the king without being asked to come see him, she would be punished by death. Mordecai reminded her that she is also a Jew and the law applied to her as well. And then he also reminded her that God would save His covenant people with or without her. But maybe God put her in this royal position to be used to save His people. So after praying and fasting, Esther agreed. She is well known for her bold statement:

> *"I will go to the king, though it is against the law, and if I perish, I perish."*
> **ESTHER 4:16B**

And she went to the king and was received with favor. Esther hosted a few feasts for the king and Haman, and the truth came out: Haman planned the death of Queen Esther and her people! The king was outraged, and Haman was punished by death. Because the Persian law didn't allow the king to take back Haman's law, the king told Mordecai to make a new law that said the Jews could fight against their enemies on the appointed day. Of course, the Jews fought and defeated their enemies. God's covenant people were safe! Even though God isn't mentioned a single time in the book of Esther, there are so many clues that show us that He was in control. It was not random that Esther and Mordecai didn't return to Jerusalem. It was not luck that Esther became Queen. We can trust in His perfect control over the smallest details of our lives! But when we think of Esther, we should also think of Jesus. He is the true and better Esther in that even though Esther was super brave and risked her life to save her people, she did not end up perishing. She even remained Queen. But Jesus came to earth knowing He was going to perish to save His people. Jesus said, "When I perish, I will perish"! God saved His covenant people from Haman's evil plan through Esther, and God saves all of His children according to His plan through Jesus.

PRAY TOGETHER AS A FAMILY

Dear God,

Thank You for being in control of the big things in our lives and the little things in our lives. You hold the universe together, but You also hold the cares of each of our hearts. We can trust in You! And thank you, Jesus, for leaving your heavenly throne to come to earth as a baby to save us. You knew You would perish, yet You came anyway. Thank You for saving us!

In Jesus' name we pray,
Amen

1. God is not mentioned in the book of Esther, but we saw how He was in control of the details to save His people. How does that show us that He is trustworthy?

2. How does Esther's story relate to the Abrahamic covenant? (Hint: it's about God's covenant family!)

3. Esther said "If I perish, I perish" but Jesus said "When I perish, I will perish." Jesus knew that He was coming to die for us on the cross. How does that stir your heart to love Him more?

VISIBLE GOD

Esther and Mordecai were Israelites that remained in Susa, one of the capitals of Persia. But throughout that time, there were many Israelites that moved back to Jerusalem. They came in three waves, and the key leaders were named Ezra and Nehemiah. These men taught the Israelites about God's law for them. You see, it had been 1,000 years since the law was first given, and most of the Israelites didn't know what it said. The Israelites were excited to follow God's law, but it wasn't long until they messed up again. They needed new hearts! And only God can transform someone's heart, and He does it through the Promised Savior, Jesus! And this is how one of the last stories in the Old Testament ended. Afterward, the Israelites experienced 400 years of silence. God didn't speak through prophets and there were no miracles, but of course, we know that He was still in control of all that was happening in the world. And a lot happening! Ever heard of guys like Plato and Aristotle and Alexander the Great from your history books? Their lives fell in this silent time that is called the intertestamental period.

The story picks up in the New Testament with a man named John the Baptist. And John the Baptist was called by God to tell everyone the good news—the Rescuer was coming soon! His message was pressing: turn away from your sins and turn toward God. This is what we call repentance. He was saying, "Get ready!" And guess what? Jesus came just as He said He would! His people had waited generation after generation. But in that time of waiting, God was faithful and kind, and He gave His people many hints that the Promised Savior would come. Again and again, He showed His people that they could trust Him to fulfill His grand plan. And then, it happened. An angel spoke to a young girl named Mary, and he told her that she was chosen to carry the miracle baby – the long awaited Savior. The angel told her this:

> *He will be great and will be called the Son of the Most High,*
> *and the Lord God will give him the throne of his father David.*
> *He will reign over the house of Jacob forever, and his kingdom*
> *will have no end.*
> LUKE 1:32-33

Hearing this, Mary was confused. Joseph wasn't her husband yet, so how could this physically happen? They were ordinary people! How could they have the Son of the Most High that would rule a kingdom? The angel told her that it was all God's work—the Holy Spirit would do it. And guess what? Mary believed the angel. And soon enough, Jesus, the Son of God, came quietly as a baby. And He came exactly the way God told His people in the Old Testament that He would come from the tribe of Judah (Gen. 49:10) and in the town of Bethlehem (Mic. 5:2) from the line of David (Isa. 9:6-7) by a virgin (Isa. 7:14). You see, Mary's soon-to-be husband Joseph was from the tribe of Judah and the line of David. Mary was a virgin. Jesus was supernaturally conceived by the Holy Spirit. At the time of Jesus' birth, Mary and Joseph were in Bethlehem. They didn't lived there, but were there because the Roman emperor told the Jews to go back to their hometowns for a census, which is a way to count people. Bethlehem was Joseph's hometown. You see, not a single detail was a coincidence. God was and is in control, and this is just His grand plan unfolding!

Jesus came quietly as a baby, but God magnificently announced the occasion with a blaring star in the sky. And He sent an angel to tell the good news to some shepherds that were out in the fields nearby. The Messiah is born! And a choir of angels sang, "Glory to God in the highest heaven, and on earth peace to those on whom his favor rests!" (Luke 2:14). And these ordinary shepherds went to Bethlehem and saw with their very own eyes the fulfillment of the Promised One—Jesus! He came just as He said He would.

PRAY TOGETHER AS A FAMILY

Dear God,

Thank You for who You are. You are faithful and trustworthy. You are good and kind. You keep Your promises, and You sent the Promised Savior, exactly the way You said You would. Thank You, Jesus, for humbly coming as a baby. You came to do what we could never do. Like the angels, may we worship You. Glory to God in the highest!

In Jesus' name we pray,
Amen

1. Jesus came into the world exactly the way God said He would. How does that grow your love and desire to know God's Word?

_____

_____

_____

_____

_____

2. God's plan was unfolding perfectly, and we see it again in the birth of Jesus. How do the details encourage you to trust Him and His plan?

_____

_____

_____

_____

_____

_____

3. Why is the birth of Jesus good news for us?

_____

_____

_____

_____

_____

_____

Way, TRUTH, AND THE Life

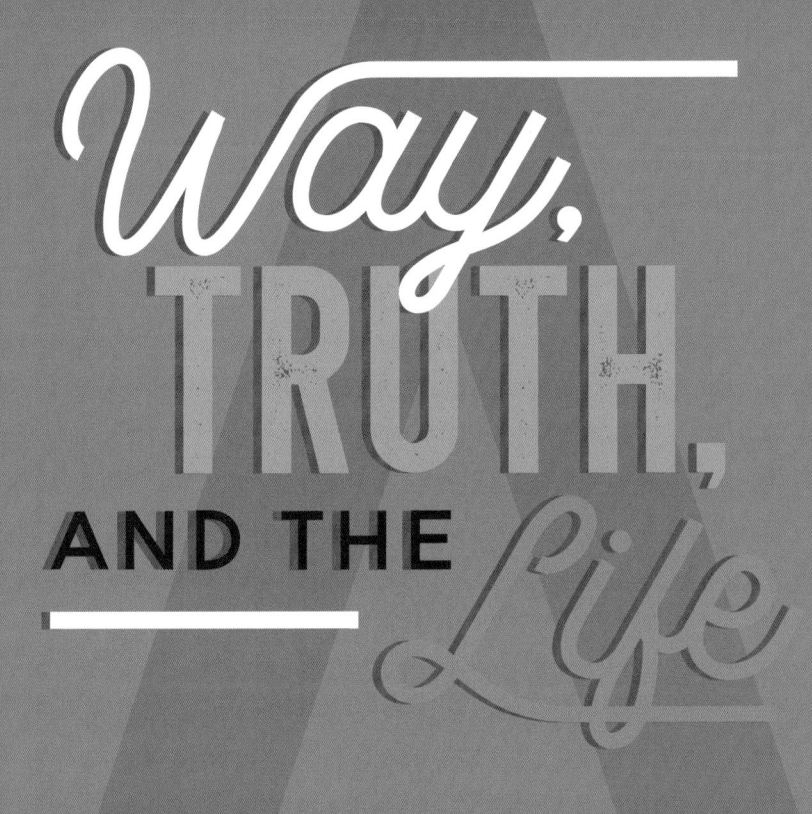

Jesus is why we celebrate Christmas every year! It's all about Him who is both fully God and fully man. Jesus was fully human. He was born in a manger. He was a baby that had the same needs that any other newborn baby has. He was also fully God. He was born sinless and angels declared His glory at His birth. It is so important that we believe that Jesus is God in human flesh because only then could He satisfy God's wrath on the cross, which is what our sins deserve.

And this is exactly why He came to do what we never could. He lived a perfect life, which He could only do because He is the Son of God. In human flesh, Jesus embodied every aspect of God's character (Col. 2:9). He was perfect and holy. His worst enemy could not even accuse Him of wrong! He had divine attributes and performed divine acts. But He lived quiet and unseen for 30 years in Nazareth. The Bible simply says that He grew strong and wise and had favor with God and man (Luke 2:40, 52). It was God's beautiful design to have Jesus grow mentally, emotionally, intellectually, and physically as a normal human develops over time.

His public ministry began after His baptism. Baptism was a symbol of confession and repentance of sins. We practice the same today. After we have acknowledged Jesus as Lord and Savior, we are baptized to publicly say that we belong to the people of God, the true Israel. But why would Jesus, who was completely sinless, need to be baptized? You see, this was an act of obedience to God the Father and His will. And Jesus showed us that He also loves His people so much that He was willing to do things to identify with sinners and to show people the right way to live. And when Jesus was baptized, God said this, "You are my beloved Son, with you I am well pleased" (Luke 3:22). Immediately after this affirmation from heaven, Jesus was led by the Spirit to the wilderness to be tested by Satan (Matt. 4:1). We know, of course, that Jesus didn't sin or disobey. He really is holy and righteous! And He didn't even show off His divine power to overcome the enemy. He used Scripture to fight off the lies, and He trusted in God's love and provision. And this is exactly what we are to do when we face temptations, too.

JESUS DIDN'T SIN OR DISOBEY. HE REALLY IS HOLY AND RIGHTEOUS!

Jesus' earthly ministry was according to God's plan. After Jesus' time in the wilderness, He soon went to Galilee, and it was there that He called His disciples. The Jews in Galilee were not as traditional as the Jews in Jerusalem. They were more open to Jesus and the gospel. But ultimately, this was exactly what the prophet Isaiah said would happen 800 years earlier. Isaiah prophesied that "the people who were sitting in darkness saw a great light" (Isa. 9:2a). Everything was according to God's grand plan! And wherever He went, Jesus preached with authority. He was always available, tender, and loving. And His main message never wavered. It was always about God's kingdom and His offer of deliverance from sins to those that believed in Jesus. Yes, Jesus miraculously healed many. He even raised people from the dead! But His words alone proved that He was the Messiah. Jesus' mission on earth was to "seek and save the lost" (Luke 19:10).

THE CROSS WAS HIS GOAL. HE WAS THE MESSENGER AND
THE MESSAGE. HE IS THE GOOD NEWS!

At the very end of His earthly ministry, Jesus told His disciples this:

Jesus told him, "I am the way, the truth, and the life. No one comes to the Father except through me. If you know me, you will also know my Father. From now on you do know him and have seen him."

JOHN 14:6-7

JESUS IS CLEAR - HE IS THE ONLY WAY TO GOD.
THAT WAS TRUE BACK THEN, AND IT IS TRUE TODAY.

PRAY TOGETHER AS A FAMILY

Dear God,

You are in control. Jesus was always the plan. Thank You, Jesus, that You are fully God and fully man. Thank You for coming to do what we could not do. You lived a sinless life. You displayed perfect obedience. You joyfully submitted to the will of the Father. You are the way, the truth, and the life. You are all we need. Thank You!

In Jesus' name we pray, Amen

1. Jesus was fully man and fully God. Why is that important to know and believe?

_____

_____

_____

_____

_____

_____

2. Why do you think it was God's plan to have Jesus live quietly for 30 years? What can we learn from that?

_____

_____

_____

_____

_____

_____

3. The gospel is exclusive. Jesus alone is the way, the truth, and the life. How does this message differ from what the world says about religion, faith, and the afterlife?

_____

_____

_____

_____

_____

_____

X-MAS TO THE CROSS

Have you ever seen anyone write Christmas as "X-mas"? What's that about? In church history, the X was actually a symbol for the name of Christ. This is because when the Greek alphabet is translated into the English alphabet, the first letter of the Greek word Christos is actually the English letter X. So to use shorthand, some people mark X to represent the word Christ. And if you tilt your head a bit, an X looks like a cross, right? When we think about Jesus Christ, we should always remember the cross.

Did you know that more than half of the passages in the New Testament regarding Jesus' earthly ministry focused on the last week of His life? So naturally, we should ask ourselves, "What happened that week that was so important?" It really was the most important week in the history of the world. Some churches call it Holy Week. It starts with Palm Sunday. This is when Jesus journeys into Jerusalem, and the crowds are praising Him by shouting, "Hosanna to the Son of David!" (Matt. 21:9). They recognized Jesus as the Messiah. They even created a pathway for Him with palm branches and their own clothes to say, "Yes, He is royalty! He is the King of the Jews!" They had their own expectations of what this long awaited Promised Rescuer would do to bring peace and victory to the Israelites. But Jesus knew exactly what would happen, and He knew it had to happen this way. So as He entered Jerusalem on a humble donkey, He fulfilled yet another prophecy that was proclaimed 500 years earlier (Zech. 9:9).

HE WAS ALSO DECLARING THAT HE IS THE PEACEMAKER, BUT IN ORDER TO BRING TRUE PEACE, HE NEEDED TO DIE TO GIVE HIS LIFE AS A PAYMENT FOR OUR SINS.

But they couldn't see beyond their own expectations of how the promises should be fulfilled. You see, a few days later, the Israelites would look to a sacrificed lamb to symbolically die for their sins because it was Passover. It was tradition. But they didn't understand that Jesus was going to be the Passover Lamb, crucified at the exact time lambs are slaughtered to cover the sins of the people. Jesus was the true and better Passover Lamb, and He had told them this would happen. He would save them from their most desperate need—spiritual death due to their sins. But they were looking to Him to establish a kingdom right then and there. They were looking to Him to save them from the oppression of the Roman Empire that was in power. They wanted their own definition of peace on earth. After all, wasn't that what the Old Testament said He would do? This was what they had in mind of the Messiah—not the cross.

But the cross is the climax of this grand story of redemption that God wrote before He created the world. It is the crossing point of two things: the greatest expression of God's love for His people and the greatest display of man's wretchedness and sin. So yes, Jesus died on the cross, just as He said He would. He endured humiliation and the worst physical pain, but

more than that, He faced the wrath of God for our sins. But He is the good news! Three days later, the tomb was empty. He is risen just as He said He would! He was alive again in a transformed body that was witnessed by over 500 people! And after 40 days, He ascended into heaven and now sits at the right hand of God the Father.

But He's coming back again. He is the King of Kings! And when He does, we will have our own resurrections that will unite us with Jesus. We don't know when He'll return, but we can trust that He will come back and He will be right on time. And in our season of waiting, our lives should be marked by holiness and godliness (2 Peter 3:11). We can wait with hopeful expectation that He will come back to gather His children!

God—his way is perfect; the word of the Lord is pure.
He is a shield to all who take refuge in him.
PSALM 18:30

PRAY TOGETHER AS A FAMILY

Dear God,

Thank You, Jesus, for the cross. In the cross, we see Your greatest expression of love for us. You did what we could not do, and it was God's plan from the very beginning. And we believe in Your resurrection. The tomb is empty! And we believe You will come back again to gather Your children. You are the King of Kings!

In Jesus' name we pray,
Amen

1. On Palm Sunday, the Israelites were celebrating Jesus as the Messiah and King of the Jews. What did they expect Jesus to do in Jerusalem?

_____

_____

_____

_____

_____

2. A few days later, they supported the crucifixion of Jesus. Jesus knew this was the way it had to happen. It was not a surprise to God! What is the role of the cross in God's story?

_____

_____

_____

_____

_____

3. Three days later, the tomb was empty! Why is the resurrection important?

_____

_____

_____

_____

_____

YOUR MISSION

We have seen throughout the Old Testament that Jesus was on every page, and the overall message was, "The Messiah is coming!" Then, Jesus did come exactly how God told us He would come. Then the message changed to, "He is here!" He lived a perfect life and accomplished His mission on the cross. He defeated death in His resurrection and is now seated at the right hand of God the Father. But where are we in this storyline? You see, just as God sent Jesus on a mission, Jesus sends us on a mission. He said it clearly in John 20:21, "As the Father has sent me, I also send you". Did you realize that Jesus had a mission for you? What is Jesus talking about here? Jesus said this to His disciples after He was crucified on the cross. He had defeated death and rose again. This is what we call the resurrection. God the Father raised Jesus by the power of the Holy Spirit! Jesus was alive again. He had a transformed body, but the marks of His wounds from the cross were still there. It was really Jesus! And He showed Himself to over 500 people, including His disciples. There really is no doubt about the resurrection of Jesus!

But when He met the disciples after the resurrection, He gave them this mission. He sent them out into the world to spread the gospel. You see, Jesus came to "seek and save the lost" (Luke 19:10). His mission was to save sinners! You see, sinners are lost because they are dead in their sins (Ephesians 2:5). This is why the cross was the reason why Jesus came to earth at all! And this is what separates Christianity from other religions. Our God sought us! He came down to us to make a way back up to Him! This is why Jesus said:

> *I am the way, and the truth, and the life. No one comes to the Father except through me.*
> JOHN 14:6

Followers of Jesus don't have to figure out a way to get to God. Jesus is the way! And that's our mission today—to tell sinners that they can be reconciled to God through the life, death, and resurrection of Jesus. Our mission is the ministry of reconciliation. Now, that's a big word, but it just means that humans and God can be together again. Now His people are to tell everyone about it. This is why we are on this earth today. Reconciliation is your mission. You don't have to save anyone, but your job is to tell people about Jesus and the truth that only He saves. You and I are ambassadors of Christ, which just means we represent Him in a foreign land. We don't make up our own message and go in our own authority. No, we share the good news of Jesus Christ (the gospel) and go under the authority of Jesus who sent us!

Back when Adam and Eve disobeyed God and took a bite from the tree of the knowledge of good and evil and sin entered the world, God didn't say, "What did you do?" No, God walked in the Garden of Eden, and He called out, "Where are you?" God was seeking them because He is a seek-and-save God from the very beginning. And He found them and told them the gospel. He told them a Rescuer would come and make a way for human beings to live in God's presence again. And as we know, the Rescuer is Jesus and He did come and make a way!

NOW WE GET TO TELL OTHERS THE GOOD NEWS OF THE GOSPEL:
JESUS CAME TO SAVE SINNERS. JESUS MADE A WAY.

PRAY TOGETHER AS A FAMILY

Dear God,

Thank You, Jesus, that You came to the world to seek and save the lost. Help us to be ambassadors for you and tell other people about who you are and all that you have done. Help us to make disciples and bring glory to You.

In Jesus' name we pray,
Amen

1. Jesus' mission was to "seek and save the lost" (Luke 19:10). Who are the lost?

2. What is our job in the mission and what is God's job?

3. Our God is a seek-and-save God. What stories have we read that showed us this aspect of God?

Zion

So when will this mission be completed? What's the end of the story? Like with any book, it's important to know the ending! God, who is the divine author of this grand story in the Bible, knows the final chapter. It hasn't happened yet, but God gives His people glimpses of what will happen at the end. God tells us in the Bible that Jesus will come back. We are waiting for Jesus' second coming. He won't come as a helpless baby this time. No! He will come as a powerful judge. From Genesis to Revelation, there are so many passages that say Jesus will return to rule over His glorious kingdom. This hasn't happened yet. Remember, His first coming ended with the crucifixion, resurrection, and ascension. At this very moment, Jesus is seated at the right hand of God the Father. God is crystal clear that Jesus will come again.

For the Lord has chosen Zion; he has desired it for his home: "This is my resting place forever; I will make my home here because I have desired it.

PSALM 132:13-14

God will establish a new heaven and a new earth. It will be even better than Eden, remember? This is called the New Jerusalem, and it will be where God dwells with His people again. It won't be like the old Jerusalem where God was just in the Most Holy Place in the temple. No, there will be no physical temple because "the Lord God the Almighty and the Lamb" will dwell in the city with His people (Rev. 21:22). You see, the people of God are called the church and called the bride of Christ. In the New Jerusalem, they will dwell with Him forever with no separation because they will be completely pure. It will be a beautiful place with no tears, wars, death, pain, or sin. The city will not even need the sun or moon anymore because "the glory of God illuminates it, and its lamp is the Lamb" (Rev. 21:23). Can you imagine that?

If you have put your faith in Jesus as your Lord and Savior, this is your future. In this season of waiting for His second coming, you can wait with hope and great expectation. Only God knows when Jesus' second coming will happen, but we can live in peace with this glorious eternity in mind. And in our waiting, we can worship God by doing everything to the glory of God. We can grow in our love and knowledge of Him through prayer and the study of His Word. We can worship and fellowship and lovingly serve others with our local church. Don't forget—we are ambassadors of Christ, continuing God's mission by telling others the good news of Jesus. We can work hard in the waiting because we know we will dwell with God in the New Jerusalem one day and that is the end of the story.

FROM GENESIS TO REVELATION, THERE ARE SO MANY PASSAGES THAT SAY JESUS WILL RETURN TO RULE OVER HIS GLORIOUS KINGDOM. THIS HASN'T HAPPENED YET. REMEMBER, HIS FIRST COMING ENDED WITH THE CRUCIFIXION, RESURRECTION, AND ASCENSION. AT THIS VERY MOMENT, JESUS IS SEATED AT THE RIGHT HAND OF GOD THE FATHER. GOD IS CRYSTAL CLEAR THAT JESUS WILL COME AGAIN.

Dear God,

You know all of the details of the end of Your story. We may not fully understand everything, but we can be sure of this: Jesus will return again! Just as it was said in Genesis 3:15, God wins and Satan loses. Your people will dwell with You forever in the New Jerusalem, and there will be no separation, tears, pain, wars, death, and sin. Thank You, Jesus! In our waiting, may we live faithfully as Your ambassadors and joyfully tell others the good news of Jesus.

In Jesus' name we pray,
Amen

1. Even though we may not know all of the details of the end of the story, we can know for certain that Jesus is coming back as a righteous judge. If Jesus is your Lord and Savior, you can be confident that Jesus has forgiven all of your sins and has given you His righteousness. Have you put your faith in Jesus?

2. The greatest part of the new heaven and new earth is that God will live with His people again. There won't be a physical temple in the New Jerusalem! Instead, how will God dwell with His people?

3. As believers, we shouldn't sit around and do nothing until Jesus returns. What are we called to do in the waiting?

UNDER GOD'S *Control*

VISIBLE GOD

Way, TRUTH, AND THE *Life*

X-MAS TO THE CROSS

YOUR MISSION

Zion

Thank You

for studying God's
Word with us

CONNECT WITH US

@thedailygraceco
@kristinschmucker

CONTACT US

info@thedailygraceco.com

SHARE

#thedailygraceco
#lampandlight

WEBSITE

www.thedailygraceco.com